PRAISE FOR *READING*

Kenny cares for his students and the stories ᴛʜᴀᴛ ᴛʜᴇʏ about the power of narrative, he guides us through a rich seam of strategies and ideas for developing the reading habit and deepening children's inner world. Surely, this book will speak to every English teacher's heart – the possibility of growing a love of reading that will last long after the school gates have slammed shut.

Pie Corbett, teacher, author and storyteller

Reading for Pleasure is a clarion call to teachers, librarians, school leaders and even parents to make much of reading because it matters so much to the present and future lives of our children. This book is rich with evidence, pragmatic insights and practical strategies to enhance reading for pleasure. Read it for pleasure, then act upon it with purpose.

Alex Quigley, English teacher, author of *The Confident Teacher*

This is no bombastic ego-driven polemic designed to gain notoriety or attention for the writer but a genuine exploration of what it is that prevents young people from engaging with reading and, importantly, what we can do to help break down these barriers. Kenny offers ideas and suggestions but doesn't ram these down your throat or at any point suggest that he is the font of all knowledge, preferring instead to share what's worked for him and see if you might like to try it. Everything from reading programmes to e-readers is discussed fairly and carefully, with seventeen years of experience of both readers and the act of reading in mind, by someone who clearly holds the written word dear and wants to open up the beauty of it to all.

Colin Goffin, Executive Vice Principal, Inspiration Trust

A blistering, honest, thought-provoking and funny read. Only Kenny could write about something so important yet still manage to reminisce about the likes of Kenny Dalglish, Bill Hicks and Debbie Harry along the way and even equate the Greek philosophers to the *Godfather* actors! I can't recommend this book highly enough.

Tait Coles, Assistant Principal,
Head of ITT across a group of schools in Bradford

Reading for Pleasure is a great antidote to some of the common problems surrounding reading in schools today. In the last twenty years, the world we live in has dramatically changed. When I was growing up in the 1980s, I could have easily read a whole book in the time it took a game to load on a computer. That was the Sinclair Spectrum for you! Today, students have instant access to games, films and other media. So, how do you get students to read books in the modern age? How do you get students reading in an age when you can have an instantly engaging experience at the click of a button? Thankfully, Kenny has some practical, easy-to-use and sensible remedies.

Chris Curtis, Head of English,
St John Houghton Catholic Voluntary Academy

Reading for Pleasure is packed with good ideas and suggestions, many of which I shall pass on to others with the recommendation that they read Kenny Pieper's book. Within 24 hours of reading it, I found myself quoting him in front of several hundred teachers. It is so refreshing to find a book written with such clarity by a practising teacher and this book reads as though Kenny is there, with his coffee, beside you in the staffroom, talking to you.

Ros Wilson, education consultant and author

Kenny Pieper is the English teacher you wish you had. Wise, funny, quietly encouraging and patient, Kenny's prose makes for a comforting accompaniment into what is both a memoir and a call to arms. Bigging up reading's an easy win with teachers, but not so much with disgruntled Glaswegian teens. We could argue about whether the 'for pleasure' part matters all that much – maybe the ability to read is more important than the desire to do so – and if there were a sure-fire formula for getting people to do things they didn't want to do then its discoverer would surely rule the world. But, if anyone can, Kenny can. This is a useful and, dare I say, pleasurable addition to any teacher's bookshelf.

David Didau, education writer and speaker

Kenny shows how, with 'time, patience and love', teachers may plant seeds which will flourish in the year to come. This is a book for all teachers – not just English teachers, and it is not just about fiction – and it powerfully communicates the central message that, 'creating the environment for children to become readers who read, because they enjoy it and value it, must be the backbone of any education.' All teachers and trainee teachers, in all subject areas, whatever their level of experience, could benefit from reading it – and to do so will be a pleasure.

Jill Berry, former head teacher, leadership consultant

A humorous and human take on both a personal and practical issue facing our young people today. Kenny is able to articulate the problem of our 'sweetcorn kids' with his impassioned take on things, offering interesting and engaging approaches to challenge the issue. Supported by a wealth of experience and his own very personal journey to becoming a reader, he lays the foundations for a future generation of pupils to engage with their world. Viva la reading revolution!

Samantha Bainbridge, Key Stage 4 English coordinator,
Our Lady and St Bede Catholic Academy

HOW TO TEACH

a passport to everywhere

Reading
for Pleasure

KENNY PIEPER
EDITED BY PHIL BEADLE

 Independent Thinking Press

First published by

Independent Thinking Press
Crown Buildings, Bancyfelin, Carmarthen, Wales, SA33 5ND, UK
www.independentthinkingpress.com

Independent Thinking Press is an imprint of Crown House Publishing Ltd.

First published 2016. Reprinted 2017.

Edited by Phil Beadle

British Library Cataloguing-in-Publication Data
A catalogue entry for this book is available
from the British Library.

Print ISBN 978-1-78135-267-0
Mobi ISBN 978-1-78135-269-4
epub ISBN 978-1-78135-270-0
ePDF ISBN 978-1-78135-271-7

Printed and bound in the UK by
Gomer Press, Llandysul, Ceredigion

ACKNOWLEDGEMENTS

To every kid who has ever walked into my classroom and listened to me rattling on about reading, I thank you. You make me a better teacher every day. To my colleagues in the English department of Duncanrig Secondary School who tolerate me, while shining brightly, raising the bar of every pupil who walks through our door and helping them achieve more than they thought they ever could, I thank you. To Phil Beadle, who took a punt and whose late night tweet, along with priceless sweary editing and encouragement, made this whole thing possible for me, I thank you. But, most of all, to Elaine. My heart, my soul, my life. Without your unconditional support and faith in me, I could never have got here.

FOREWORD BY PHIL BEADLE

Shouting about how good you are seems to me a sign of little more than insecurity and immaturity. There are a lot of people in British education using channels to let everyone else know how good they think they are. If they were really so free from the lacerating self-doubt that nightly plagues them in their sleepless and sweaty beds, they wouldn't be showing off quite so obviously, and self-praise, as my dear old mum would say, is … well, y'know.

Social media, and specifically Twitter, is a distorting mirror that can turn us into Calibans. There are those who use it to boost their careers, those who use it to display the plumage of their egos, those who use it to be disagreeable and there are those, like Kenny, who use it to learn, to make friends, to find out things that will make them a better teacher than yesterday.

Kenny is a mature and developed adult who understands that part of the responsibility of being a man is to behave with quietness and with strength, to question inherited opinion, to devote one's self to something outside of that self. He is a devoted teacher to the students he serves and understands that keeping things simple is a work of great intellectual complexity. I admire him and think him a better man than myself.

His book is, I think, much like the man himself, a quiet and understated gem. It is a human work glittering with empathy. Kenny recognises the part that a love of reading has played in his own transformation from blue collar worker to white collar littérateur and holds a hand down to younger humans so that they might use reading in the same way that he has: to transform their circumstances and their outlook, to enrich their experience of being alive by communing with the human frailties, doubts and poetry of others who have recorded their souls on paper. In working on this book together, we have been very much in symbiosis: two working class adult males trying to pass on a tradition that we both benefited from greatly, making obscure gags about seventies footballers, having an occasional lighthearted swear up. I regard Kenny Pieper as the epitome of decency and a valuable and engaging (and engaged) voice on a subject of profound political importance. After reading this book, so will you.

Phil Beadle

CONTENTS

Chapter 1

BOOKS AND ME

It was contagious! Seventy pages![1]

I BLAME ALEX DICKSON

Back when I was a lad, before the Internet and the Twitter and the Facebook, I had nothing but a little silver radio to keep me company. With one tiny white earphone to stick in my ear, I would listen to the local station, Radio Clyde, every night as I drifted off to sleep. It was a different time; don't judge me. On certain evenings, Alex Dickson would talk to me in the strangest, deepest, most exotic (but still unmistakably Glaswegian) accent about books: strange adult books, detective stories, historical fiction, biographies. I totally and utterly fell in love with them.

The fact that adults could have conversations about such things was a revelation to me. We had books at home when I was growing up – not many: some encyclopedias (my dad is American so we had the curiously extravagant *Encyclopedia Americana*), the odd novel, piles of *Whizzer and Chips* and *The Broons* annuals. It would be unfair to say we were not a reading family: there were books, I had seen them; but on 'Alex Dickson's Bookcase', the host and his guests would talk about them for half an hour. They informed me, not about any one book in particular, but about a whole world of reading. Each week, at 10 o'clock, the sound of Jimmy 'Schnozzle' Durante singing

---

1   Jimmy Durante, '(I'll Never Forget) The Day I Read A Book'.

'(I'll Never Forget) The Day I Read a Book' signalled a strange kind of heaven to me: a heaven that would change my life forever. Here was a life of books!

So, from there, how did I go on to become a reader? Certainly not from being forced through some half-baked reading scheme at school. My earliest book-ish memories are of visiting the cavernous town centre library in East Kilbride with my pal, Gerry, and staring in awe at the covers of the 'Alfred Hitchcock and the Three Investigators' series, debating the merits of the Famous Five over the Secret Seven and, well, just being in a library. Long before the emer-gence of big windows and airy freedom, before coffee and computers, we would sit on a jaggy green carpet reading for hours. I even recall early on in secondary school skipping school dinners to sit in the library flicking through *The Guinness Book of Records*, dropping sausage roll crumbs into the pages. Pub quiz colleagues would thank me years later.

> George: I'm gonna read a book. From beginning to end. In that order.
>
> 'The Summer of George', *Seinfeld*[2]

I take the act of reading for granted. Perhaps you do too. You've picked up this book and you're reading it comfortably enough. During the course of the first chapter you may even begin to read the signs that I'm a strong cham-pion of reading for pleasure. If you were in my classroom, I might ask you to read my lips to make sure you knew exactly where I'm coming from. If you couldn't, I might have to keep you behind and read you the riot act. You may well be reading between the lines and getting the gist of what I'm saying already. Reading isn't a problem for you, is it? Do you read me?

At this point, you may be able to read my mind and understand that reading is a serious business. You should know that by now. You've read the fine print.

---

2 'The Summer of George', episode 22 (season 8), *Seinfeld*, dir. A. Ackerman (originally aired 15 May 1997).

The point is that reading as a concept is part of our everyday wardrobe, our language, our existence. You've always read; you do it as naturally as breathing or eating.

However, the word 'reading' itself doesn't have the same connotations for everyone. I teach kids for whom the mere mention of reading causes them to shrink like a salted snail. They sneer and smirk and avoid it at all costs; inside they cringe and cry. The ubiquity of the word 'reading' in our lives makes it easy for *us* to assume it's not actually that big a deal, but what about those who do find it a challenge? Their lives are terrifying obstacle courses of reading related problems. They know they struggle with reading. Everything that happens in their day-to-day existence reminds them of this. They know that not being able to read well differentiates them from most of their peers. It leaves them isolated and lost. And we know it too.

A WORLD OF WONDER

Tom sits cross-legged in the library. He's not a reader, never has been, and I can see this is difficult for him. It's not only that he doesn't like reading or doesn't like this particular book; he finds reading difficult. It's difficult because he really wants to please me, his new English teacher, in the first week of his new term in his new school. He wants to like it – he really does – and he concentrates hard so as not to move his lips as he reads. He wants to read 'A Series of Unfortunate Events' by Lemony Snicket because his friend liked the books, and he watched the movie over the summer and quite liked it too. He can't do it though. He can't really read, you see.

Tom is probably representative of hundreds (maybe thousands) of kids going through the same thing that week. What have we done to him? He is 11 years old and has lost, or never discovered, the joy of submerging himself in a book. He's had seven years of school and is sitting and hoping forlornly that it will all click into place for him. Until that happens, he'll feel excluded from an amazing world: a world his friends inhabit comfortably.

He won't wander the dark and ancient corridors of Hogwarts; he won't leave Rivendell side by side with Bilbo Baggins, an imaginary backpack stocked for the journey; he won't climb through the wardrobe into Narnia or fight alongside a young James Bond. And something about that doesn't sit right with me. As an English teacher, it breaks my heart to see kids like Tom who, through no real fault of their own (perhaps they are victims of circumstance), have missed out on the opportunity to fall in love with books. I'm not blaming anyone aside from a system that appears to have failed him. For what greater gift can we give children than the ability to read well?

No role model exists at home for them. Every time we ask them to read they may smile and go along with us, but – like the opening scene in *WarGames*, where Mr Blonde from *Reservoir Dogs* and Leo from *The West Wing* have to turn their keys at the same time to launch a nuclear missile[3] – the keys ain't turning. They freeze and nothing happens. No reading inspired bombs go off. And they leave school, not merely unaffected by this strange reading thing, but saddled with a great deal of emotional baggage about being an outsider, even more entrenched in a belief that reading is for others more intelligent than them.

We need to step up and be their reading mentors, getting involved in their lives, or at least be the ones who will properly encourage them to turn the key. It won't happen by accident; it won't happen if we just leave them to it.

---

3   *War Games* (1983), dir. J. Badham.

TRIPS DOWN AMNESIA LANE

You'll remember the days when all of your friends would gather at school and discuss the progress you'd all made with that difficult Dickens novel you'd agreed to read by the end of the month. The fall-outs and arguments over whether Jane Eyre was a victim or a heroine. Whether Thomas Hardy could ever stand up to Jane Austen. No? Me neither. The problem English teachers have is that we forget that developing a love of reading is a process, not a switch. It takes time. When we assume that children will read simply because we ask them to, when we accept that some of them, well, they just ain't readers, and give up on them, then we may be embedding a stigma that will stick with them forever. We can chuck piles of cash around on elaborate reading schemes, but unless we get involved in their reading we're leaving it to chance, and that's not a chance I'm happy to be any part of.

MY LIFE WITH BOOKS

I love being around books. I love the way they look on the shelf: their spines lining up in rows, increasing in length throughout my life. I love the idea that I can hold all of *The Lord of the Rings* or the complete works of Shakespeare in my hand. I love the mess of them as they pile up on my desk. I love seeing other people reading them on the train. I love them second hand in charity shops and brand new through the post. Still do. My wife doesn't have to look too far if we lose each other in a busy town centre. I'm to be found in the bookshop spending good money on books I may never get round to reading.

The first thing I look for when I'm invited into the homes of others is a bookcase. That's the true way to judge a person's character: I check out what they read. If there's no bookcase then I give you permission to turn around and run; run like the wind and never look back. Save yourself. Don't be a hero and try to save your friends. Time is of the essence here. You have no place in this person's world. For a house without a bookcase filled with books is not a house; it is a vacuous den of reality TV and the Xbox. Nothing to see here. At best you're condemning yourself to a lifetime of brainless dinners in this place, counting your life away discussing the moistness of the chicken. At worst, you could end up marrying this cretin. Don't think twice.

If there is a bookcase then head straight for it. Pretend to be listening to your host's light conversational openers, perhaps have a salt and vinegar crisp or a sausage-on-a-stick as your eyes glance sideways at the books on offer. The deal hasn't been sealed yet. They could still let themselves down. At this point, you're on your own. If it were me, I'd be looking for some serious literature on that shelf. Not necessarily things I've read, but a clear sign that this is not the bookcase of an idiot. The autobiography of a politician? Maybe. The autobiography of Gary 'set the' Barlow? Get out of there!

Of course, if I spotted some Philip Roth, Marilynne Robinson, P. G. Wodehouse or Orwell, I'd be looking around and wondering where I'll put my records when I move in. The point is that what we read forms part of the person we become. Like it or not, readers are judgemental. Regardless of how hard we try, adult non-readers are a strange animal, more often than not to be avoided.

KIDS TODAY, EH?

We seem to be too accepting of a society that has stopped reading, or at least stopped seeing reading as being something important. In this book, I want to argue that we too easily take our children's reluctance to read as something we can do nothing about. We shrug our shoulders, raise our eyebrows and say, 'Well, what can you do?' Even if it were true that kids no longer read – and I'm not convinced this is the case – as educators (or those interested in reading for pleasure) surely it's our duty to do something about it. To rekindle a love of reading for kids, to provide them with a route to improved literacy and an end to what might well be a generational problem of poor reading skills – a cycle which leads to and embeds poverty, lack of opportunity and an ever increasing wealth gap. Reading changes lives; of that I have no doubt. It changed mine.

In a previous life, I was unemployed for over two years during the Thatcher-led eighties. Eventually, I would work on factory floors, in shops, in a hospital; I worked for months on night shifts and twilight shifts, as well as 9 a.m. to 6 p.m. day shifts, barely getting by. What I remember from those days is not the work I did, because it was difficult to differentiate one day from the next. I recall some great friends and some great laughs, but nothing whatsoever about the jobs I did. Mostly I remember what I read.

I read every day. Every lunch break. I spent time in bookshops and libraries. I read reviews. I wasn't university educated, but I could see this was something important. This was a life. A year of night classes from Monday to Thursday got me to university, and I never really looked back. The first in my family. It was reading that got me there. I could only have been an English teacher. Now I work in a building that has a library. How perfect is that?

THE DAMAGE WE DO

I wanted to write this book to share some of the strategies I've used in classes over the years, but also to raise some issues about the manner in which we, as teachers, help to create, even embed, negative attitudes to reading. Lack of choice, lack of good books when there is a choice, lack of time to read in school, lack of care. Together with a culture where reading for pleasure has become an extravagant extra in the classroom, we are in the midst of creating a national scandal, a potential minefield.

The Read On. Get On Campaign claims that, rather than raising achievement for all, 'Our education system too often entrenches disadvantage and inequalities.'[4] Think about that for a minute. Then think about it for another minute. We have been unable to change this situation. For many generations – in Scotland anyway (I don't know what the hell was going on elsewhere) – we have voted Labour in the hope of some working class reawakening, placing our trust in a political system that, surely, had our best interests at heart? But our education system just isn't working for those who need it most; those who are screaming out for a break and a way in to some sort of normal, comfortable life; those sweetcorn kids who we spit out at the end of a ten year period little better prepared for the rest of their lives than when they entered the system.[5]

In all likelihood, we'll never see the revolution we have hoped for during most of our lives (the end of guffawing posh boys telling everyone else to tighten their belts), but we can help to create a generation of kids who will be able to tell when they're being shafted. Too often, we vote for those who will impose their political ideologies on us because we fail to engage in the detail of the debate. We don't read newspapers; we don't know about the intricacies of the economy; we accept things too easily. We even resent those who protest on our behalf because they cause trouble and block our streets. So, maybe, by creating the conditions for our students to become good readers – that is, readers who read because they choose to, readers who question, readers who think – then we can, at least in some small way, prepare them for the life of political oppression that is to come.

---

4   Read On. Get On Campaign. *Read On. Get On: A Mission to Ensure ALL Children in Scotland Are Reading Well By 11* (London: Save the Children, 2014). Available at: http://www.savethechildren.org.uk/sites/default/files/docs/Read_On_Get_On_Scotland.pdf, p. 3.

5   Sweetcorn tends to leave the system in the same form as it entered. Don't think about it too much.

Rather than concerning ourselves with the vaporous gibber of '21st century skills', we need to get our young people reading and enjoying reading. The kids who sit in front of you and me in our classrooms every day could well be future teachers, doctors and lawyers; a child in your Year 6 class at the moment might by the girl who cures cancer; the boy next to her might invent something that solves global warming. So shrugging your shoulders and harrumphing, 'What can you do?' just doesn't cut it.

I began writing this book in the midst of the greatest political and cultural shift in Scotland in my lifetime. In 2014, 16- and 17-year-olds were given the vote in the referendum for an independent Scotland. We were told that young people weren't mature enough to take that vote responsibility; we were told that they didn't care; we were told that they wouldn't take it seriously. But, do you know what? They did all of those. They got involved in the political process for the first time in their lives. They read up on the important issues, discussed them among themselves and others and, for the most part, took their responsibility seriously. The referendum saw one of the highest turnouts in any national referendum in modern history.[6] And look what happened: the greatest political transformation in a generation.[7] Okay, we'll have to wait and see how much genuinely changes, but involving young people in the process and giving them the opportunity to read up on the issues and discover how powerful they can be is hugely important. It can bring change, even on a local level. So let's not underestimate the importance of getting our young people to read.

6 Electoral Commission, Scottish Independence Referendum: Report On the Referendum Held On 18 September 2014. ELC/2014/02. Available at: http://www.electoralcommission.org.uk/__data/assets/pdf_file/0010/179812/Scottish-independence-referendum-report.pdf, p. 1.
7 It also turns out that 71% of 16- and 17-year-olds voted to leave the union. See J. Burn-Murdoch and A. Wisniewska, Scottish referendum: who voted which way and why?, FT Data (19 September 2014). Available at: http://blogs.ft.com/ftdata/2014/09/19/scottish-referendum-who-voted-which-way/.

AND IF THEY DON'T READ?

What scares me rather more than the admittedly borderline unlikely possibility of a generation of illiterate kids is the rather more real possibility of them being what Donalyn Miller describes as 'aliterate': a generation of kids who can read perfectly well but who choose not to.[8] In a sense, illiteracy is something we can tackle. We may not be particularly good at tackling it at the moment – in a recent government-financed Scottish Survey of Literacy and Numeracy it was discovered that, while literacy levels are high in Scotland (80% of all 12–13-year-olds performed well or very well in reading), that percentage had dropped over the previous five years.[9] But our politicians are, seemingly, willing to throw money at the problem. They just haven't been very successful thus far.

When it comes to adults we find similar problems with literacy. Research completed by the Scottish Government found that 'around one-quarter of the Scottish population (26.7%) may face occasional challenges and constrained opportunities due to their literacy difficulties, but will generally cope with their day-to-day lives; and within this quarter of the population, 3.6% (one person in 28) face serious challenges in their literacies practices'.[10]

Aliteracy seems to me to be somewhat different. People who can read, but choose not to, make an active choice to disengage from political reality. They have not been convinced of the importance of reading in their lives. What difference does it make to them? If we fail to answer this question for them

---

8   Donalyn Miller is a legendary teacher from the United States who focuses on getting kids to read. I came across her book, *The Book Whisperer: Awakening the Inner Reader in Every Child* (San Francisco, CA: Jossey-Bass, 2009), in a bookshop in New York and it changed my life. It is the book I would recommend to everyone; after reading this one, of course.

9   See Scottish Government, Scottish Survey of Literacy and Numeracy 2014 (Literacy). Statistics Publication Notice. Available at: http://www.gov.scot/Resource/0047/00475898. pdf.

10   See http://www.gov.scot/Topics/Education/Life-Long-Learning/17551.

in school, then we create a generation of passive citizens unwilling or unable to take part in the political process.

You have to wonder about a system which, after 50-odd years of free compulsory education, has failed to narrow the literacy gap between rich and poor. Despite the necessity of schooling in their lives and the teachers who tell them that education will help them to get a better job, young people often see older brothers and sisters ending up in the same low paid jobs as their parents and grandparents. And the cycle continues. What could reading give them that would change that?

I grew up in a working class culture that was wary of 'cleverness' and made every attempt to remind us that we should know our place. Anybody with illusions of grandeur was quickly slapped down. I sometimes hear parents, heart-breakingly, mock and dismiss their own children at parents' evenings, unable to understand the educational possibilities open to them: 'I kent yer faither ...'[11]

The idea that schools impose perceived middle-class values on children might be part of the problem; after all, we convince ourselves that all children should have the dream of university and a lifetime of debt. Reading is something that only 'clever' people do, isn't it? Of course it isn't. But that is the scale of the challenge at times. We're not merely trying to develop a reading habit in our students, but we're asking them to consider a cultural change: one that may well be alien to them and their families. We ask them to dream of a future which is also alien. We dismiss their values (or, at least ask them to hand them in at the door), their fast food diets, their clothes, their TV shows. So, when our fancy-shmancy education fails for them, it becomes all the more challenging next time round.

---

11   Literally, 'I knew your father,' but the implication is, 'I know where you come from, so pack it in with the airs and graces, pal, or you'll get a slap.'

This is why I think it is essential that we spend more time focusing on encouraging a love of reading at the expense of almost everything else we do as teachers. This doesn't necessarily need to mean a love of fiction. Every subject teacher needs to encourage kids to read about their subject and to provide high quality reading materials that interest them.

Kids who read well, read well across the curriculum and are in a more advantageous position to succeed in school and in life outside of school. Reading widely as a habit, rather than as an imposition, gives us the opportunity to build up our background knowledge and develop those reading skills, to increase our understanding of the world, to move on to more challenging work. It becomes part of what we do rather than what we have to do. I really believe that those who see themselves as readers – and I make a distinction with those who merely read – become more active students, and will become more active citizens and, one fine day, the thoughtful, intelligent, hard-working people we want them to be.

BOOK WHISPERING

I learned from Donalyn Miller, the writer of *The Book Whisperer*,[12] that I had to be involved in my students' reading, and not just at the end with a hopelessly malformed review or a terribly busy poster. These things serve no real purpose. It's important to allow and encourage students to respond to their reading, and I'll suggest some of the ways I get them to do that later in the book. But posters are merely time-consuming and entirely shallow reflections of their reading. They keep students busy. There may be a space for some form of book review, but writing one after reading a great book is the last thing any sane person would want to do. It mixes up a whole load of

---

12 Please read it. I can't recommend it enough.

writing problems with reading, and you don't want that in the early stages if reading for pleasure is your goal. From this day forward, promise that you will never, ever ask a student to write a book review. Swear it! There ... we have progress already.

Forget about written responses to their reading for the moment and engage with them. Should they want to talk about what they've read, then create the conditions for them to do so. We need to be by their sides when they encounter confusion or want to share their excitement or laughter at the funny bits. They want us to do that. Too often we don't.

Reading for pleasure seems to be the first thing that slips off the desk when the pressure is on but, as English teachers, we must not forget why we are there in the first place. We loved reading and books and talking about reading and books. What happened to us? Why do we forget the thing that got us where we are? As another American educator, Kelly Gallagher, states: 'When schools deprive students of the pleasures of recreational reading we end up graduating test takers who may never read again for pleasure.'[13]

We need to follow up our beliefs in reading, not let tests and deadlines take over. If your students are only reading when they are being tested on it – either in essay form, close reading or interpretation – then they will begin to see that for what it is and stop reading altogether.

I grew up in the same town in which I now teach. I teach kids who live in the very streets I ran around in as a child. I went to school with some of their parents; I kent their faithers. But, often, I feel distant from them. I became a teacher because I wanted others to have the same opportunities I had; not to become better than their parents, not to rise above the class in which they grew up, but to take full advantage of the education on offer to them.

---

13 K. Gallagher, *Readicide: How Schools Are Killing Reading and What You Can Do About It* (Maine, NY: Stenhouse Publishers, 2009), p. 45.

To show them that kids from those streets don't have to spend their lives in low paid jobs and struggling to survive.

The intention I have in writing this book is to set out some of the ways I have tried to do this through reading. It's a huge, often impossible, task. But I think we owe it to the kids we teach to ensure that reading provides them with the same chances in life that we've had.

Chapter 2
TEN MINUTES

WHAT CAN YOU DO IN TEN MINUTES?

I became an English teacher because books changed my way of thinking about the world. I was politicised by *The Grapes of Wrath* and by much of Orwell's work; I was knocked sideways by Alasdair Gray's *Lanark*, amazed that books could be written about my home city of Glasgow in such a challenging and refreshing way. Reading set me on my way to being the first member of my family to go to university.

I teach in Scotland and see each of my classes for four periods a week (five times in the fifth year – Year 12). Like all English teachers, I'm required to cover a load of stuff that sits in the yearly planner: touching all the bases in reading, writing, talking and listening, while ticking all of the Curriculum for Excellence boxes too.[1] So to commit time to allowing my students to read

---

1   Curriculum for Excellence is the now 12-year-old curriculum in Scotland which, to say the least, has had its problems. What started from what I call an 'eight word manifesto' – the four capacities of 'successful learners, confident individuals, responsible citizens, effective contributors' – has developed into an overly assessed, box-ticking nightmare at times. The original plan states: '*Curriculum for Excellence* aims to achieve a transformation in education in Scotland by providing a coherent, more flexible and enriched curriculum from 3 to 18.' It explains that 'The curriculum is the totality of experiences which are planned for children and young people through their education, wherever they are being educated.' Scottish Government, *Curriculum for Excellence. Building the Curriculum 3: A Framework for Learning and Teaching* (Edinburgh: Scottish Government, 2008). Available at: http://www.educationscotland.gov.uk/learningandteaching/thecurriculum/ whatiscurriculumforexcellence/index.asp, pp. 3, 11. We had hoped to de-clutter assessment but it now has more ticks than a mangy dog.

for pleasure – free choice reading, if you like – is a big commitment. But what do I expect back?

Ten minutes. Every day. Some kids who come to me from primary school have never read a whole book on their own. Many leave their year with me having read four or five. The cumulative effect of only ten minutes of reading every day turns them into readers. So it's worth it, isn't it? What else can you do in ten minutes? I ask parents this question at parents' evenings and, after the initial uncomfortable giggling, usually get similar responses: walk to the local shop for a paper, have a cup of tea, relax during half-time at the football, listen to three songs on your iPod. So, *providing* – and I use that word deliberately – ten minutes for every single pupil to read whatever they like can be transformative over time. What I try to get across to parents and their kids in my classes is that reading for ten minutes a day – to start with anyway – can change their lives.

But why ten minutes of reading and not fifteen, or five, or seven? It's a judgement call. I had to consider the limited time I had with my classes each day. Ten minutes at the beginning of the lesson is a great settler for classes and it ensures that even the most reluctant readers will do forty minutes of reading a week. As an alternative to the dreadful 'reading period', which seems to be designed to get it over with and give the teacher a little break each week, it proves to be far more beneficial. Incidentally, it has been shown that small bursts of regular reading are more effective than sporadic longer sessions.[2]

In the sobering report, *Read On. Get On*, the authors claim that 'As little as ten minutes a day can make a big difference in a child's life.'[3] As long as it is

---

2   M. Lewis and S. J. Samuels, Read More, Read Better? A Meta-Analysis of the Literature On the Relationship Between Exposure to Reading and Reading Achievement. Unpublished manuscript, University of Minnesota, 2005, p. 24.
3   Read On. Get On Campaign, *Read On. Get On*, p. 22.

coupled with reading instruction, then all sustained silent reading leads to improvements in fluency and understanding.[4]

THE READING ENVIRONMENT

I expect every child to read and respect the reading space of others, and I do this by creating a reading environment. What might that be? Quite simply, it is a place where reading is expected. Even if you're not particularly into it today, you must respect the reading space of others for those ten minutes. Many of them might never have seen an adult reading quietly, never mind any of their peers. They must learn what this means and what it looks like.

At the beginning of every lesson, students enter the room quietly –often they will meet me standing at the classroom door, reading. They quietly get their books out and start reading. There are no questions. They must not interupt my reading or anyone else's. Silence. Ten minutes every day. So, if they're not prepared or have forgotten their book or finished it, they know what to do. There is a class library (see Chapter 3) if they've finished their book overnight, or they can update their dialogue reading journals (see Chapter 4). Either way, they must not interrupt the reading of others. That's my starter. Every time.

It can be a slow process but eventually they get the hang of it. The younger ones, especially, need the time to develop and grow into this habit: they can come from primary schools still with a need for attention and validation from their teacher, so ignoring them for ten minutes can be a challenge initially.

---

4   Lewis and Samuels, Read More, Read Better?, p. 7.

MAKING A DIFFERENCE

In his 2002 memoir, *Teacher: The One Who Made the Difference*, Mark Edmundson, a professor of English at the University of Virginia, touchingly recalls the book that changed his life. He had been a high school football player. He lived for sport and never really enjoyed the academic life – until he discovered Ken Kesey's *One Flew Over the Cuckoo's Nest* in the library:

> I read in a rage that so much that was palpably my business had been kept from me. It's like finding that the post office has for years been siphoning away packet after packet of the most engrossing letters – some of them approaching love letters, no less – addressed personally to me. And who has been guilty of this malfeasance? Who are the corrupt officials? The faculty of Medford High are the main conspirators.[5]

There had not been a single moment in his time at school where he was encouraged, allowed or left to read what he wanted to read. Kesey's tale of the evils of institutionalisation hit home as he recognised that there were books out there, outside of the school curriculum, that were *for him*. Edmundson would spend the rest of his life catching up with that time, reading everything he could get his hands on: 'A line by the poet Richard Brautigan summed it all up: My teachers could have ridden with Jesse James for all the time they stole from me. I read it and wept, angry tears sliding over my face and down onto the bucking mustang.'[6]

A similar young boy in my class failed an assessment last year, disastrously. He was a disengaged kid: likeable but uninterested. While I had hoped that he would have passed the paper comfortably – he had made some great progress that year – he barely completed half of the questions. What I later

---

5 M. Edmundson, *Teacher: The One Who Made the Difference* (New York: Vintage, 2002), pp. 251–252.

6 Edmundson, *Teacher*, p. 252.

discovered was that, during the assessment, he had been reading Nick Hornby's *Slam* underneath the desk. This boy had definitely not been a reader at the beginning of the year; in fact, he actively fought against it. He read for the first ten minutes of every lesson, as do all of my classes up to S4 (Year 11), and I was secretly very proud of him. (He did pass the follow-up assessment so untwist those knickers.)

Should I have been more observant? Probably. Should I be proud of him? Definitely. And while he may never become a professor of English at Highbrow University, this boy is a reader, and I'd like to think that has something to do with me. The class was challenging for many reasons – I laughed and cried over them. We had some magical moments and some horrible ones too. But I persisted with ten minutes of reading at the beginning of each lesson. Even when pressures of coverage, resistance to any reading from some and, at times, open hostility from others made it extremely tempting to give up and do something else. It would have been easy to admit defeat, but my memory of Mark Edmundson's experience kept niggling away at me. If not me, then who? If not now, then when? If I didn't make that extra effort to persuade them to read, then who would?

WHAT BLOODY GOOD IS READING ANYWAY?

To write, publish, or distribute a book is like putting a message in a bottle and tossing it into the sea: its destination is uncertain.

Gabriel Zaid[7]

Of course, it is essential that our children find their own message in their own bottle. Children growing up in book-free homes are already playing catch-up in the literacy stakes at a very young age, and that gap widens over time. Our propensity to build on prior knowledge means that the more literate kids continue to develop at an accelerated rate, while those without a strong base of vocabulary acquisition fall further behind. When children grow up in homes in which some words are not heard, never mind read, they fail to develop the ability to form stories and sentences, to connect syntactical structures. As Maryanne Wolf observes:

> The importance of simply being talked to, read to, and listened to is what much of early language development is about, but the reality in many families (some economically disadvantaged, some not) means that too little time will be given to even these three basic elements before a child reaches the age of five.[8]

It is not my purpose to delve too far into the minutiae of early reading development – as a secondary teacher this would be disingenuous of me – but it is a sobering thought that when children arrive at secondary school many are already miles behind their peers. In Scotland alone, as of November 2014,

---

7   G. Zaid, *So Many Books: Reading and Publishing In An Age of Abundance*, tr. N. Wimmer (London: Sort of Books, 2004), p. 100.

8   M. Wolf, *Proust and the Squid: The Story and Science of the Reading Brain* (Cambridge: Icon Books, 2008), pp. 103–104.

22% of children were growing up in poverty.[9] Poor literacy skills merely further entrench these disadvantages and inequalities. We are not necessarily ignoring the problem, but we are missing opportunities to put things right. The startling statistic that over half of children from the most deprived areas leave primary school not reading well should shock us more than it does.[10] But it doesn't, does it? Certainly, it doesn't shock us anywhere near enough to get appropriately angry about.

Remember that creating church schools to allow children to read their own bibles also allowed them to think about what was in these bibles and to further cogitate, 'Hey, wait a minute ...' Why would we want to make that mistake again, eh? The wilful failure to address the political nature of literacy means that whole swathes of our children grow up marginalised and not understanding many of the ideas that competent readers take for granted; hence their irrelevance to the political classes and their demonisation in the media. Literacy opens doors and creates successful lives. If not dealt with, what is initially a difficulty develops into an identity.[11]

SMALL STEPS

Parental involvement has perhaps the most powerful influence on a child's reading.[12] However, when children turn up at school having been without positive reading role models for so long, what should a teacher do? The

---

9   Read On. Get On Campaign, *Read On. Get On*, p. 3.
10 Read On. Get On Campaign, *Read On. Get On*, p. 6.
11 See T. Newkirk, *Holding On to Good Ideas In a Time of Bad Ones: Six Literacy Principles Worth Fighting For* (Portsmouth, NH: Heinemann, 2009), p. 105.
12 See Department for Education, Research Evidence On Reading for Pleasure (May 2012). Available at: https://www.gov.uk/government/uploads/system/uploads/attachment_data/file/284286/reading_for_pleasure.pdf, p. 22.

difficulty of encouraging reluctant readers to confront this issue is something we can too readily underestimate, because the child in front of us will have deeply engrained and embedded negative attitudes towards reading that will take time, patience and, damn it, love, to overcome.

Hopefully, we can begin to understand that, as English teachers meeting 11-year-olds for the first time, we can start to develop a greater empathy for those kids who struggle. When, unconscionably and offensively, we point a finger at primary school teachers who have been unable to overcome literacy problems, when we lose patience and, heaven forbid, when we give up on young kids who claim to 'hate reading', understanding where those difficulties come from can help us target the areas where we might begin to form a solution.

As adults and teachers, we tend to unthinkingly mythologise our own reading histories. Our formative years with books tend to become hugely important to us: we'd like to think they were spent reading *The Wind in the Willows* in a tree house or strolling along the riverside contemplating Thomas Hardy's difficult later works. The likely truth was probably somewhat different. I must have given up on loads of books before I found the one that finally got me. Beyond the usual suspects I was studying at school – *The Great Gatsby*, *Of Mice and Men*, *Lord of the Flies*, *Macbeth* and so on – I struggle to remember the one book that hooked me on to reading, so I try to keep that in mind when encouraging my pupils to choose books.

I try not to impose 'good' books on young readers at first. My newly acquired middle-class values are not necessarily helpful at this point. Free choice in reading is massively important for all children, especially for kids who struggle with reading in the first place. So I let them read 'Captain Underpants' books if they want to (initially). Once you get them into the habit, then you can start to slide more challenging material across the desk at them.

READING AS AN UNNATURAL ACT

Mythologising our own reading histories might seem a comfortable thing to do when we're adults, but it rarely helps when we want children to read for pleasure. Reading is not a natural act. 'We were never born to read,' says Maryanne Wolf,[13] but we do create meaning from images, and we try to form stories and narrative from what we see in our environment. It is sobering to consider that, in asking children to read, we are, rather than merely asking them to do something they should be doing, asking them to do something which doesn't come naturally to any of us.

Babies are born with the ability to both see and speak. From birth, we make sense of the world through the faces and the objects we experience. We express our emotions through sound in reaction to what we see and what we feel about things. Reading, on the other hand, is far from preprogrammed. How could it be? Letters are merely symbols; since Fred Flintstone left Barney Rubble rude messages about Betty on the cave wall, we have attempted to communicate through our own brand of hieroglyphics. So it stands to reason that reading is a hugely complex business.

Daniel Willingham argues that 'We think of reading as a silent activity – consider a hushed library – but sound in fact lies at its core.'[14] When we read, we create sounds through images and transfer them into speech. If we struggle with the symbols, then we struggle with necessary coding skills to make sense of anything. Barney had to have some sense of what Fred was attempting to communicate in order to be offended by his friend's playful mockery. And this has serious implications for the young child learning to read. 'We are capable of reading before we can actually read',[15] but it takes

---

13   Wolf, *Proust and the Squid*, p. 1.
14   D. T. Willingham, *Raising Kids Who Read: What Parents and Teachers Can Do* (San Francisco, CA: Jossey-Bass, 2015), p. 7.
15   A. Manguel, *A History of Reading* (New York: Penguin, 2014), p. 35.

time and a whole lot of complicated thinking to create strong, independent readers.

An array of mental skills is required. Firstly, for Barney to get the joke, he'd have to understand the individual symbols used by Fred and be able to sound them out in his prehistoric noggin. Then, he'd have to piece them together to form words. A slow Barney wouldn't quite get the joke yet, but he may put those words together and form them into sentences which make sense. As he becomes more confident, those sentences might become paragraphs. Fred's in trouble now.

All the time Barney is attempting to hook all of this on to his current knowledge – what he knows about the world, about Fred, about Betty, about himself. Without that prior knowledge, every symbol, every letter, every word is a challenge. If we want Barney to be a confident and skilled reader, then we'll want him to see beyond the text: 'the goal of reading is to go beyond the author's ideas to thoughts that are increasingly autonomous, transformative, and ultimately independent of the written text'.[16]

For Barney to get Fred's message, and to understand it (in an instant, as well as good readers do), there are many complex machinations going on in the brain. So much prior learning has been undertaken to make reading a seemingly instinctive act, such that it becomes, as Alberto Manguel claims, 'almost as much as breathing ... our essential function'.[17]

And this is where teachers come in. The importance of linking reading to existing knowledge is essential if we are to convince reluctant readers that there is a point. As a secondary school teacher in Scotland, my youngest pupils come to me at ages 11 and 12 in S1 (Year 8). They have had seven years of primary school during which they will have read several class books. They may well be, and often are, experienced readers with stories to tell. But

16   Wolf, *Proust and the Squid*, pp. 17–18.
17   Manguel, *A History of Reading*, p. 7.

what of the others? The ones who come to me with nothing, no reading histories to speak of?

The idea of an 'interest inventory' came from Steven Layne.[18] It allows me to tap into the prior knowledge and experience of my students, at the very least providing me with a foothold on to something that might begin to build a reader. You can call it an interest inventory or you can call it what you like. The hand-out consists of a series of questions which ask students to tell me about their lives – their hobbies, passions, favourite books and movies, dreams, anything you think might be interesting really; it's totally up to you. I tend to hand this out during the first week of term and, when completed, I keep them in a ring binder to which I can refer throughout the year.

Interest inventory

Name _____

1   What do you like to do in your spare time?

2   Do you belong to any clubs or teams? If so, what are they? If not, why not?

3   What kinds of movies do you like? Why?

4   What are your favourite sports? Why? There can be more than one if you like.

5   If you had three wishes what would they be?

6   What kind of books do you own?

---

18   See S. L. Layne, *Igniting a Passion for Reading: Successful Strategies for Building Lifetime Readers* (Maine, NY: Stenhouse Publishers, 2009).

7   If you had a surprise day off from school, how would you spend it?

8   If you could transport yourself to any time or place in the past, where would you go?

9   If you had the chance to meet any famous person, living or dead, who would it be? Why?

10 If you could pick any three books from a bookshop for free, what would they be about?

11 If you could go on a trip to any place in the world today, where would you go?

These pupil profiles prove to be useful in lots of ways throughout the year. They can be your best friend at moments of greatest resistance, when you feel that you're making no progress and are about to give up on that difficult pupil with whom you are struggling to connect. The knowledge that he or she likes Superman comics, or surfing, or ponies might be a wee conversation piece later in the year. It's a fantastic way of beginning to build a reader if they've nothing much in terms of foundations to build on. When the 'I hate reading' child is your target, you can find a book on a topic from their inventory, a magazine which reflects their interests or even a current newspaper article.

Thomas Newkirk, a teacher at the University of New Hampshire and author of *Holding On to Good Ideas In a Time of Bad Ones*, tells a tale of his very early years of teaching, and finding it impossible to get his disaffected class of boys to read anything other than the sports section of the newspaper. His dad tells him to travel around the town buying every copy of *Sports*

Illustrated he can get his hands on, if that's what it takes.[19] He did so and, after finding articles which would hopefully be interesting, he had a class who were beginning to read. Not voraciously at first, but it was a start. The point being that you need to move heaven and earth to get something into their hands they can read. It won't be easy, but it will be worth it.

A DYING ART

If you are an English teacher and you are contemplating dropping library or reading time because that essay needs finishing, please don't. I beg of you. Be patient and you could, perhaps, change someone's life.

I had originally wanted to give this chapter the ironically intended title, 'The Dying Art of Reading for Pleasure' (as I don't believe it is dying, in fact). Go into any high street bookshop and you'll see that book sales are flourishing. Head to the young adult section and you'll see an explosion of new titles and new genres. Our passive acceptance that children don't like reading and won't like reading, and the fact that we convince ourselves that it's difficult and time consuming to encourage them to do so, because we have so much else to cover in class, is as much to blame as anything else. As a secondary school teacher of English, it is not merely my job to develop young readers in my classroom but my duty; to assume that it isn't my responsibility is nothing short of criminal.

I return to Mark Edmundson and his resentment and anger towards his school when he realised that, by failing to provide him with the opportunity to read and take the time to get great books into his hands, he looked back on missed opportunities and closed doors. I would argue that every time we

---

19   Newkirk, *Holding On to Good Ideas In a Time of Bad Ones*, p. 178.

drop reading time for something else (some writing or even working on a class novel), every time we show our annoyance when young Tom has forgotten his book or wants to change it, every time we fail to promote reading for pleasure as the greatest thing they will learn to do in school, then we fail our students.

I have made it my biggest goal in teaching to do what I can to create lifelong readers. Reading for pleasure is what got me here; reading for pleasure got me through two years of hellish unemployment in the eighties; it got me through two lonely years living on an island in Greece teaching English to uninterested, wealthy Greek kids, after their school day, when it was scorching hot (and as I may have already mentioned, *on an island*, so isolated from any bookshops for months at a time). Books have punctuated my life more regularly and more reliably than birthdays. I remember where I was when I read *One Flew Over the Cuckoo's Nest* for the first time; I know where I was when I finished John Fowles' *The Magus*; I know how I felt when I read *The Lost Weekend* by Charles Jackson and *American Pastoral* by Philip Roth; I speed-read the last Harry Potter because I wanted to finish it before my niece. And I'm a grown man!

More crucially, reading has made me aware of the world around me. I understand more and can make more connections. If I deprive my students of even a chance of that, then I'm helping to create the legacy that leads children into a life of poor literacy skills, poor life chances and misery. Reading books shouldn't be perceived in any way as a luxury. It should never be something that is the purview of any one group in particular. The desperate imbalances in wealth and opportunity on our own island can be addressed by tackling the literacy problem, and reading for pleasure needs to be at the heart of that process.

I wanted to write this book to achieve two things: to convince any doubters that, with passion, with commitment, with time, with choice and with love we can create readers who love to read; and to provide approaches, rather than strategies, that have worked for me and continue to work for me.

Hopefully, I can convince you. But first, let's hightail it to the library ...

Chapter 3
THE LIBRARY

> Libraries generate longing. It collects in the shelves and rustles
> under the desks and zaps people like static electricity.
>
> Ian Frazier[1]

Right. We need to get a book into their hands. How? Which book? With
those damaging years of determined non-reading to overcome, which is the
book that will give them that message in a bottle?

Looking back on my own reading history, I would love to remember which
book got me. I have hazy memories of crying in my bed after reading Robert
C. O'Brien's *Z for Zachariah*: its post-nuclear war landscape far too threaten-
ingly real for a child of the seventies. 'We're all going to die and I'll be the
only one left!' Rereading it as an adult didn't have quite the same effect,
though, and to be honest, in retrospect, I can see that it wasn't that great
a book after all. But I recall the captivating, emotional power of reading it
when young. And in having that story to tell, *Z for Zachariah* became *my*
book; no one else shares that history in the same way. That book – not, in
fact, one of my favourites at all – perhaps began the process of creating the
reader in me.

So, we should not get too hung up on the quality of the books our students
read to begin with. We may cringe as they read yet another in the 'Captain
Underpants' series, 'but if the books I have read have helped to form me,
then probably nobody else who ever lived has read exactly the same books,

---

1   I. Frazier, *Gone to New York: Adventures in the City* (London: Granta, 2006), p. 87.

all the same books and only the same books as me. I am my own literary DNA.'[2] Let them read. Just let them read.

The interest inventory means you now have a whole load of weapons in your armoury: it tells you masses about your pupils – their loves and hates, wants and needs – so get to work! You are getting to know more about them every day, so tap into your skills of deduction and relationship forming and find out even more. Get on the Internet and download an article about the hobby the child loves. Give them another one. Harder this time. Then another. Find a magazine (if you're keen, buy a subscription for them). I often tell parents who are at the end of their tether that a magazine posted through their door with their child's name on it can be a transformative experience. I used to get *Roy of the Rovers* delivered every Saturday.[3] I can still hear my old man wittily shouting up the stairs, deliberately getting it wrong: 'Whose "Ray of the Ravers" is this?' Every. Single. Week. But there was a particular excitement about getting something through the post with my name on it: it hooked me into collecting things to read.

When all's said and done, never underestimate the power of telling your own story: your message in a bottle, how reading smacked you over the head, grabbed you and shook you about a bit. My classes laugh at me when I tell them my *Z for Zachariah* story, but it opens up a dialogue. They begin to recognise moments from their own pasts: books which they read over and over again, books which scared them, books which made them laugh. They begin to create their own 'literary DNA', something French novelist and creator of

---

2   S. Hill, *Howard's End Is On the Landing: A Year of Reading from Home* [Kindle edn] (London: Profile Books, 2010), loc. 2479.

3   I must have a book in me on this topic alone. *Roy of the Rovers* was one of the original (coughs) graphic novels starring superhero Roy Race. Every week, Roy would come to the rescue of his football team, Melchester Rovers, saving them from a series of out-of-town bully boys, intent on stealing the league title from them. Yes, it was a graphic novel. It really was! And who could deny a superhero called Roy.

The Rights of the Reader,[4] Daniel Pennac, describes as 'curling up at the centre of my geography'.[5]

TO THE LIBRARY!

Driving along Maryhill Road in Glasgow, many years after I last lived in the area, I was taken aback by my own reaction to seeing the local library, still in the same place, staring down in its red sandstone glory. I hadn't thought about Maryhill Library since early childhood, hadn't imagined seeing it again; indeed, couldn't have described what it looked like until the moment of driving past it when it all came back. The Scooby Doo dream sequence which followed took me back to regular trips to this strangely echoing place where I would fill my boots with Asterix the Gaul and Enid Blyton.

Libraries are incredible places. Stop and think about this for a minute …

They collect books and provide them to the public for free. They offer an otherwise out of reach education to anyone who wants it, regardless of background. You can sit there all day, if you so wish, reading the papers. This seems an amazing anachronism in an age of capitalism and commercialism. Libraries should be considered the heart of a literate society.

Wherever I've lived, home or abroad, I've always made it a point to immediately search out the nearest library. I've been in ancient libraries in Athens, I've sat for hours in a stuffy unused library on a Greek island, I've blown the dust off books in a small town in Romania. Why? Perhaps it's the comforting familiarity of having books all around me; perhaps it's the calming safety

---

4   D. Pennac, *The Rights of the Reader*, tr. S. H. Adams (London: Walker Books, 2006) – more of which in Chapter 10.
5   D. Pennac, *School Blues* (London: Maclehose Press, 2007), p. 202.

of a room full of information; perhaps it's because it is (arguably) the most important public space in any community.

The fact that, years later, I work in a building which has one of these remarkable spaces is a source of daily amazement to me. I walk through it whenever I can and take all my classes there whenever it's possible. Yet you'd be amazed at how many teachers never get there. Whether they don't see the relevance for their subject, whether it's too much hassle, whether they've never been invited or don't have the time, I can't say. But if we're to properly teach kids the importance of libraries, it's a space which should never become the sole preserve of the English department. The library in our school is a wonderful place: enormous windows from floor to ceiling, welcoming light and space for classes to spread out and read, a study corner with computers and another corner with study booths. Our previous librarian acquired huge bean bags for readers to sit on. There are glass cases displaying class work, a selection of magazines and you can even browse the yearbooks of former year groups. But still it can be a terrifying prospect for younger kids.

I mentioned young Tom earlier and we'll return to him again. He's the young lad who arrives at secondary school to find himself already locked outside of the world of the reader. He browses the shelves aimlessly, completely in the dark about where to start. And while it can be easy to feel sympathy for Tom, how much empathy do we really have as teachers? Rather than merely suggest books for Tom to read, in what sense can we put ourselves in his wee shoes? You see, giving him what we think is appropriate reading makes us feel good, but he still lacks the history required to understand why it's important.

I try to ensure that my classes go to the library at least once a week. As I've already explained, I insist that they all read for ten minutes at the beginning of every lesson, so they'll be needing a book. Many of them come to school with a book every day anyway, so they instinctively know what to do when they get to the library. Library rules are second nature to them. But some children have never been to a library and don't know how to behave.

By the end of the first visit each year, I have already recognised the four or five 'Toms' in the class, not all of them boys. Arriving in the library is like throwing them into a swimming pool when they have never been taught to swim, and natural instinct isn't going to help them here. One of them picks up a 700 page novel, the others pick up books without even looking at what they are. This is why a teacher talking about books, every day, whenever possible, is important for these guys. They need to hear what books can do, recognise what they can find in them, talk about what they might discover. They need to see us reading, picking up a book, carrying one around, being readers. There is nothing more important. As Scout says in *To Kill a Mockingbird*, when Miss Caroline forbids her from learning to read with Atticus, 'Until I feared I would lose it, I never loved to read. One does not love breathing.'[6]

So, discussing books becomes the device I use as I model the life of a reader. When we're in the library, I tell them about my reading: what confuses me, what entertains me, what makes me laugh. And I ask the same of them. Telling others about what they've read becomes part of my classroom. Recommendations fly round the room. We have book speed-dating, where students try to convince others that their book is the one their talk partner should read next (see Chapter 6). When teaching language points I reach for my current novel and discuss a particular image, the use of contrast or an effective use of the colon. As a result, Tom starts to see that reading is useful to him. He begins to enjoy his ten minutes at the beginning of every lesson. Sometimes, he'll even read for ten minutes at night and come in and talk about it. Excitedly.

As the year progresses, the library becomes *his* space too. He becomes *included*.

---

6   H. Lee, *To Kill a Mockingbird* (London: Pan Books, 1974), p. 24.

THAT FIRST VISIT

Get your new class to the library as soon as possible – on the first day of term if you can manage it. And just like modelling reading in Chapter 1, you need to model library behaviours too, along with the strange rituals the children will need to learn.

- They may need a library card. My school doesn't use them, but how students borrow and return books is something they'll need to know. The layout will become familiar quite quickly as long as you return there as often as possible, but don't underestimate the power of actually borrowing books. Make a big deal of having a library card – some may never have had one. It is special: a golden ticket to wonderful words and a mountainful of important stuff.

- Before that first visit, take time to get together with your school librarian and flesh out a plan. Get some great books out and onto the desks for your class to fight over. Create a buzz about the visits. Convince them it is a treat and a gift to visit the library. It's not merely an extension to the classroom; it's a visit to someone else's territory. We have been given special permission to take time out of class to go there, so we must use it wisely.

- You might want to construct a treasure hunt to get them all over the library: in and out of fiction and non-fiction, magazines and reference books, key texts and great novels, dictionaries and encyclopedias. The important thing is to show off the library as an amazing adventure: 'They do things differently there. We will do things differently there.'

- If you're feeling brave, run through an A–Z of books on the library shelves: I grab an 'A', do a one sentence review and, quickly and breathlessly, find a 'B', continuing on all the way to 'Z'. You may need the help of your librarian, you might even play tag team with them, but do it speedily and have a laugh while doing so. You are displaying your own joy in reading books while pulling out recommendations that your class can now borrow themselves.

Most important, though, is that the students see the library as a reading space. Senior pupils study there, staff may use it for marking, it has people coming and going all day; therefore, we need to be quiet and respect the privacy of others. Regular visits is the best way to do this. Sporadic, poorly planned visits embed the mindset that the library is not important.

THE SCHOOL LIBRARIAN

Your school librarian, as well as being one of the most important resources in your school, is probably the most scandalously undervalued. Let's not forget that these are university educated individuals who have been trained to work with books, to know about them, to know where they are and what they can do. They will set the tone for your library visits, they will prepare displays and they will look out for appropriate books for your classes. Your school librarian can be your greatest friend and closest ally when it comes to encouraging kids to read, but too often they are treated in a way that might be viewed as bordering on contempt. They are certainly not respected as much as they should be.

The library should not be used as an additional classroom space for events that ignore its special status and function: it should not be closed for exam use, for extra classroom space (although I absolutely use it to teach in) and never, ever for whole school events which are not learning related. This sets the wrong tone.

Developing a relationship with your school librarian is massively important if you are to ensure that your kids see this as an important place. This relationship provides a double-pronged attack on reluctant readers and on those who see a library visit as an excuse to mess about with their mates or stare out of the window in moody contemplation. Carsten Doig was our librarian for years and I couldn't have done my job without him.[7] We would talk for ages about our plans for my classes, when their first visits would be, which books we'd have out on display and which kids (in particular) needed more advice than others. Carsten would take the time to drop in to classes on the odd occasion and together we would create a buzz about library visits. Even though I took my classes to the library once a week *without fail*, a visit to the library became a special event, a treat even.

If there was ever a possibility of extra visits, Carsten would come down to the class and tell the pupils in person. *They* had been chosen! If he had received a delivery of new books, he would visit individual pupils who had particular interests and hand them shiny new copies. In the library, there was no doubt who was in charge. Carsten's library! Carsten's manor! The kids saw him as another teacher to talk to and someone who could find the right book for them. It worked perfectly.

Carsten would offer library passes to regular 'customers' and offer first dibs on new books to those who read most. On occasion, he and I would organise reading clubs for younger kids to come along and talk about their favourite authors or books. He would create 'banned book' displays, covering them up in brown paper bags and keeping them just out of reach. Eventually, when he'd reluctantly relent and take the covers off, the books would fly off the shelves. Boys especially couldn't wait to find out what all the fuss was about.

Being on an increasingly tight budget, Carsten would ensure that the library was stocked full of books which would be read. No fancy collections that remained untouched by human hand. Everything he bought was carefully considered. It had to be. When the annual Carnegie Medal came around,

---

7   Since replaced by the equally wonderful Liz Rowan and Louise Cooper.

Carsten would have multiple copies of all of the shortlisted senior books, ensuring my class could read them all. It was the only time of the year when my class read in groups. They voted on the book they wanted to read, joined others who had chosen that book and classwork was created around it.

In an age of austerity, where those in charge look to cut back at every available corner, it is a tragically misplaced assumption that a librarian is a luxury we can ill afford. Our school library is a beautiful space, with windows from floor to roof, but 'a library doesn't need windows. A library is a window.'[8] Carsten and all school librarians are the people who draw back the curtains.

THE LIBRARY AS A THING OF THE PAST

'What is the best gift which can be given to a community?' asked Andrew Carnegie in 1890. 'A free library occupies the first place', he declared in answer to his own question.[9] Sadly, there's a feeling that the libraries we might describe with such eloquence when recalling our childhoods are in danger of disappearing, at least as we know them. Libraries are heading for closure all across the country. Austerity measures mean that a library is perceived in certain circles to be an optional extra, and a vain one at that: an attitude that says more about those in charge and how much they value libraries and education in general than it does about the reality of cutbacks.

All over the UK, local authorities are not shy about where to look first when they need to save money. This disaster is unfolding right in front of us. And don't expect any help from the government. Before the 2015 general

---

8 S. Brand, *How Buildings Learn: What Happens After They're Built* (London: Penguin, 2010), p. 100.
9 Quoted in A. Manguel, *The Library At Night* (New Haven, CT: Yale University Press, 2009), p. 96.

election, the only mention of libraries in the main parties' manifestos was this:

> We will continue to support local libraries.
>
> We will help public libraries to support local communities by providing free wi-fi. And we will assist them in embracing the digital age by working with them to ensure remote access to e-books, without charge and with appropriate compensation for authors that enhances the Public Lending Right scheme.[10]

Read the footnote. Surprised as to which party manifesto it was in? I was. Regrettably, this was the only mention of libraries in the manifestos of any of the main parties. We all love a library, but we seem to be quite content to look the other way, to let them shrink and eventually disappear. That is what is currently happening. It's pretty clear that if you want to save your local library, then you need to get out of your chair and fight for it before it's too late.

And those poor, hard done-by library staff are also quietly being shuffled off into the archives and the stacks. Those graduates who 'just' stamp your books out or 'just' tell you how to get on the Internet are merely bodies behind a desk, aren't they? Numbers of paid staff are down 20% in the last seven years, and that's a figure that doesn't look like it's reversing.[11] Fully qualified librarians are a rarer breed than ever before.

But maybe there's a reason for that. It's easy for local authorities to see libraries as a viable target for cuts when they look at usage figures. Quite

---

10   Conservative Party, *The Conservative Party Manifesto 2015: Strong Leadership. A Clear Economic Plan. A Brighter, More Secure Future*. Available at: https://www.conservatives.com/manifesto, pp. 41–42.

11   See J. Farrington, CIPFA stats show drops in library numbers and usage, *The Bookseller* (8 December 2014). Available at: http://www.thebookseller.com/news/cipfa-stats-show-drops-library-numbers-and-usage.

simply, we are not making the same use of libraries as we did even five years ago.[12] Why might that be? Is it that books are so accessible that we no longer require libraries? Are there more book stores making books appealing and affordable? Has Wi-Fi and the e-reader made physical books less of an attractive possession? Do we devalue things that are free to the extent that we distrust them or look down upon them? Or are we merely reading less?

There is no doubt that high-speed broadband has allowed us to access information in a way unimaginable even ten years ago. Those who may have been reluctant to visit a library unless absolutely necessary now have a reason to make that absolutely unnecessary. I can answer every possible pub quiz question on my phone when I go to the toilet, so why trouble myself? It would also appear to be true that, probably since the 'Harry Potter' phenomenon, publishers have made a concerted effort to make books more aesthetically pleasing, as objects we might look upon as ornaments as much as reading material. Walk into any high street bookshop and you'll be struck by the attractiveness of books. That you can still buy a classic novel for the price of a couple of pints is also a remarkable thing. But the collected works of Shakespeare on Kindle for free? Don't mind if I do.

It's difficult to come to any real conclusion about whether we're reading less. Reports that sales of printed books have fallen[13] appear alongside the crashing of e-book sales.[14] Together with rapidly declining library use, one might

12 See A. Flood, Library usage falls significantly as services shrink, *The Guardian* (10 December 2014). Available at: http://www.theguardian.com/books/2014/dec/10/library-usage-falls-dramatically-services-visits-down-40m.

13 A. Flood, Sales of printed books fall by more than £150m in five years, *The Guardian* (13 January 2015). Available at: http://www.theguardian.com/books/2015/jan/13/sales-printed-books-fell-150m--five-years.

14 A. Trotman, Kindle sales have 'disappeared', says UK's largest book retailer, *The Telegraph* (6 January 2015). Available at: http://www.telegraph.co.uk/finance/newsbysector/retailandconsumer/11328570/Kindle-sales-have-disappeared-says-UKs-largest-book-retailer.html.

make the case that we are reading less. Hopefully this book can convince you that this is a dangerous route.

In all probability, it's an exaggeration to say that libraries will die out altogether, but we definitely have cause to worry about local access for the most vulnerable. Free access to technology is massively important if we are to close the opportunity gap: the ability to access the information available online in a library, which many of us take for granted on our smartphones, is the only opportunity some people get to contact family, friends or potential employers. Those books that we look at so fondly on our local library bookshelves will be lost to some people, books they will never be able to afford and won't ever read. That warehouse of knowledge and learning, that place where your elderly neighbour spends time during the afternoon to meet friends or read the papers – or, sadly, to keep warm – will have gone.

And we'll regret it. We might not think so until it's too late. We'll look back wistfully during pub chats about old sweets and TV programmes and we'll remember the equally obsolete libraries. Those places we went to as kids; where we read our first books; which left us in awe, not merely of the size and number of books there were, but of the reality that, no matter how much we had read, we'd hardly read anything at all. Good god, we'll regret it.

A CLASS LIBRARY

When I was first given my own classroom it had a bookcase filled with books: some classics, some unheard of, some brilliant, some awful. A good start? No, not really. They were in a dreadful state: dog eared, graffitied with every badly drawn body part you could imagine (and some you couldn't) and scrawled with the sort of insults only teenage boys can dream up. The covers were ripped or ripped off. Pupils were still being asked to choose from this second-rate selection. Is it any wonder they didn't want to read? So here's your choice. You could persist in attempting to convince Year 11 that, despite the looks (and remember what you don't judge a book by), these are great books. Or you could do what I did: get a big black bin liner, dump the sorry, broken specimens and start again. It's the only way.

I've made a point of never offering up something to a student that I wouldn't read myself, and I wouldn't have picked up those tatty old books. Of course we judge books by their covers. Always have, always will. So, even if your departmental budget won't stretch to new books, start to pick up the odd second-hand one here and there. I've even bought them with Christmas book tokens. It builds up – and you can choose the titles you want on your shelf. Get them from wherever you can, but get them.

Maryanne Wolf may be right when she claims that we are not born to read, but we do naturally like to find stories in things and create meaning in shapes and images. Watch young children as you read to them – the ones who have not had the reading upbringing some of the others have had, the ones who perhaps are not used to hearing stories, who do not read the book along with you. They stare at you, at your lips as they move and the words that come out; words which create imaginative worlds for them, words which create pictures for them, words which create meaning for them. The meaning is theirs and theirs alone. No two readers have the same reading histories.

They link those meanings to other books, to other characters and, before you know it, they're on their way.

And when we reach that moment where they take up a book to read for pleasure, without coercion, we allow them to read the same books again and again because that's what we did when we were young. There's no time limit here, no rush. We reread books we know well because we want to recreate the magic while it's still there.[15]

There are political and social ramifications if we fail to tackle the problems children have with reading, and promoting reading for pleasure in any way we can is at the heart of addressing this issue. The simple change in *your* habits – of taking them to the library and ensuring all children get at least ten minutes every day in school for reading for pleasure – will help us and them to begin to change their lives forever. It is about habit forming; it is about reversing attitudes; it is about life.

---

15 See A. Jacobs, *The Pleasures of Reading in an Age of Distraction* (New York: Oxford University Press, 2011), p. 34.

Chapter 4
TAKING IT UP A NOTCH

There are some teachers, especially those who have newly qualified, who look on parents' evenings as a special form of torture, as a version of a three hour interview for a job they've no chance whatsoever of getting. At times, it can feel a bit like being Joey Essex coming up against Jeremy Paxman: attempting to say something new and original to the parents of thirty different kids is intimidating, stressful and harrowing. 'It has been a real pleasure watching (insert name) develop this year and (insert name) is developing well, especially in writing.'

Also, there are some parents who have made up their minds about you before they've even got through the door. Their little angel has told them all they need to know, the jury has returned a verdict and, good or bad, there is often nothing you can do but grin and get through it. When the last interview is over, you sink back in your chair, swig the last sip of cold coffee and weep silent tears of relief. Until the next one. Five nights a year. Every year. Till retirement.

I've always loved them! No, seriously. I'm a bit of a talker, so to be given that captive audience, even for five minutes at a time, is a joy. As long as you genuinely know their kids as individuals I've found that, for the most part, parents are generally appreciative of everything we do for their children. Discovering the parents behind the child is one of the most important things we can do as teachers. Links home are the key to solving so many problems in schools, not least the creation of readers. I'm also in the position of teaching in the area in which I grew up, so – equally strangely and pleasantly – parents' evenings can be like a school reunion for me.

We often forget, though, that school was actually a horrible experience for many of these parents; even the idea of walking through the door can be incredibly intimidating and stressful for them. Some never got over their resentment of school (and teachers), and the structure of our parents' evenings don't do much to alleviate that. Hanging about in line for a five minute consultation, shuffling uncomfortably on plastic chairs waiting their turn; it can feel as welcoming and as enlivening as a trip to the dentist.

When it comes to reading, many may never have picked up a book (in anger) since school. They are not readers and, again, might well blame school for this – if they perceive it an important deficiency. So when we attempt to create readers in *their* children, in *their* homes, it is essential that we develop relationships with *them*. Your five minutes with them might be the only time you have to discuss reading and, if possible, convince them to take book ideas away. We must continue to nurture those links as the school years pass and, as a secondary teacher, I have the responsibility to continue the work that my primary colleagues have begun.

BOOKMARKS

So, by now, your class will have a book in their hands, they will have completed interest inventories so you know what they're into and you will have helped them to find an appropriate book. They're reading for ten minutes every day – it's a start! – and they have been to the library. But how do you know they're actually reading? How do you know they're not doing that 'pretendy' eyes-going-over-the-page thing? You've come this far, but what can you put in place that will allow you to keep the momentum going?

The bookmark I provide my students with has several functions. First of all it's a bookmark, of course. You'd be surprised how many kids merely close their books when finished and then, the next day, can't remember where they left off and then spend the whole ten minutes reading bits they've already read. Having a bookmark is hugely important: don't underestimate it. The one I have designed for them has a space for their name and their class, and on the other side there is a space for the name of the author and the title of the book they're reading. Part of the process of developing readers is allowing them to follow their own progress, and the grid on the bookmark allows them to do this. I ask them how many pages they can read in ten minutes and get them to keep the number in their heads. We then multiply that number by four – the number of lessons we have together that week. They should then double that number, allowing for ten minutes of reading homework four times a week. The final number they have will be their reading target for that week, and they write it onto their bookmarks.

Of course, some kids' targets will be different from others'. Experienced readers will fly and get through loads; reluctant readers will begin to see progress. The bookmark becomes a visual record of the amount of reading they're doing, and you can work with them on this by providing lots of praise and buckets of encouragement when they reach their targets. Each week, I ask each of them to write a short summary of what they've read that week (it only needs to be one sentence).

The most important section of the bookmark is on the right, where I ask them to get it signed once a week. This helps to create communication between teacher and parent and provides a way for parents to monitor their child's progress. I insist that they have this signed every week, especially at the beginning of the year, as it commits them to reading and encourages them to develop a reading habit using a double-pronged attack. I insist; parents insist. As the year goes on, and I'm more convinced that the habit is taking, I'll maybe ease off on the signatures. But the bookmarks stay! They get a new one for every book they read and keep them in their journals. They build up.

Title			
Author			
Agreed pages	Achieved?	Comment on this week's reading	Parent's signature

You now have a class full of readers. It will be up to you to make sure they sustain this through the habits you develop in your class.

PARENTS

I only have so much time with my class, never enough, so involving parents in their child's reading, and literacy in general, needs to remain at the centre of what schools are doing. Making that connection can have a significant bearing on how well children do in school, perhaps more than anything else. A National Literacy Trust study on the importance of reading for pleasure found that it is not merely a welcoming classroom which is essential for developing a love of reading but also home and parental involvement: 'Parental involvement in their child's literacy practices is a more powerful force than other family background variables, such as social class, family size and level of parental education.'[1]

But it's a real challenge because, often, the parents you most want to be more involved with their child's reading are those who are the most resistant. Their own bad experiences at school, coupled with the challenges of home life and all of the social difficulties that come with it, frequently make school the last place some parents want to spend time in. Structures in many schools have not changed much since my schooldays, regardless of how much we like to think they have, and I'm sure a lot of parents feel the same. So, if they have very few good memories of being pupils in what may well now be their own child's school, is it any wonder some are resistant?

We persist with hammering kids with the message that reading is important, but we need to develop effective ways of getting this across properly to parents too. Daniel Willingham describes parent–child workshops which could be a starting point for the delivery of this message: 'an initial parent–child event that has nothing to do with reading at all but is meant only to establish school as a welcoming place'.[2] If there is any possibility of delivering lessons which parents can be invited to, perhaps at open evenings, then that is helpful too. You may not get everyone to attend but you'll get some of them, and that's a start! You could also create reading newsletters, ensure that you are drumming the message in at parents' evenings, send book lists home and encourage parents to buy books at Christmas just to have them in the house. Start a revolution!

The Read On. Get On Campaign report that 'A study of 27 nations ... found that children growing up in homes with many books get three years more

1   E. Flouri and A. Buchanan, Early father's and mother's involvement and child's later educational outcomes, *British Journal of Educational Psychology* 74: 141–153, cited in C. Clark and K. Rumbold, *Reading for Pleasure: A Research Overview* (London: National Literacy Trust, 2006), p. 21.

2   Willingham, *Raising Kids Who Read*, Bonus Appendix, p. 2.

schooling than children from bookless homes, independent of their parents' education, occupation, and class.'[3] Sending children home with books is great; having them lying around the house, as part of the furniture, is way better. Teachers often take this for granted and do not do enough to ensure that it happens.

It would be amazing to be able to assist parents in becoming reading models, but that might be a step too far for some. Clearly, households that have books and where everyone reads helps to develop literate kids – 'Children whose parents reported that they read with their child "every day or almost every day" or "once or twice a week" during the first year of primary school performed higher in PISA 2009 than children whose parents reported that they had done this "never or almost never" or "once or twice a month".'[4] But for others it is a constant struggle. Schools need to be at the heart of the support systems that provide literacy instruction and reading materials. If not us, then who?

So, with their regular reading sessions you now have your class reading every day, the bookmark they have ensures that everyone has reading homework and parents are involved in the process. What now?

READING DIALOGUE JOURNALS

We must acknowledge that our little schemers can be expert at pretending to read (reading is perhaps one of the most difficult things to force someone to do and then to be sure that they're doing it). Their eyes may move over the page, but how do you know they're taking anything in? Responding to reading can be another barrier for reluctant readers, especially in writing, but

---

3   Read On. Get On Campaign, *Read On. Get On*, p. 14.
4   Department for Education, Research Evidence On Reading for Pleasure, p. 23.

there are ways. Part of the process of developing readers includes the manner in which we ask them to take responsibility for, not merely what they are reading, but also what they are learning from that reading as well as how they reflect upon it.

Nowadays, I have to bite my tongue whenever I hear about book reviews and the frivolous wastes of space that are book posters and drawings of the main character. Early on in my teaching career, I was guilty of asking my classes to write pages and pages on books they'd read, because I was sure that this would prove they had read and understood their books. I'd written them at school, and it hadn't done me any harm, had it? Damn sure it had! I hated doing them and the teacher hated reading them. Getting kids to do ream upon ream of pointless writing about books is one of the most effective ways of turning kids off reading at school. Some boys, especially, will resist reading if they're convinced that they will be asked to write a review at the end. Such writing is a huge burden on our time and achieves very little of any worth for our students. We can assess writing in far better and more helpful ways, and we can check for understanding of reading in more appropriate ways too.

Asking kids to complete a poster on their reading is pitiful and lazy teaching: it is busy work and accomplishes nothing. It may look nice on your classroom wall for a few days, but within weeks it will curl up and die like a Christmas tree in the garden of a tired dad. The further the book drifts away from their memory, the more out of place the poster looks on the wall: like an old friend who has outstayed their welcome and neither of you remember why you had invited them or what you had in common in the first place.

That said, it's unfair not to offer some form of reading response. Readers take different things from different books, and part of my own learning about how children read has stemmed from tapping in to that understanding. I came upon the idea of a 'reading dialogue journal' in Teresa Morretta and Michelle Ambrosini's book, *Practical Approaches for Teaching Reading and*

Writing in Middle Schools,[5] which I picked up in a second-hand bookshop in Glasgow. There's nothing overly complicated about it. It's merely a class notebook which passes between teacher and pupil.

What's really great about it, and what makes it so effective, is that the reading dialogue journal allows each pupil to reflect on their own reading at their own pace. Ideally, they write in it once a week, replying to a series of questions from the teacher, and this continues throughout the year. Responses need not be much longer than a single paragraph (which is great for the less able) but can continue for as long as the student wants (which is great for the creative and confident). On the chosen day, students arrive in class with their journal and quietly get down to constructing their responses. The brilliant thing is that each one is a very personal response. Every child gets to feel that you are talking to them individually.

I start every journal with a 'Hi John' or 'Hi Julie' and end with 'Mr P'. I encourage them to do the same, and it's amazing the things they get to tell me about their reading experiences. As the weeks pass, each pupil's journal develops in different ways. Some become detailed and profoundly personal: I've had kids tell me about sharing reading with their parents and even include mum or dad's response in the journal. I've also had very limited responses from weaker readers which has allowed me to further encourage and support them.

It's the dialogue part that really works. Having 150 students in and out of my classroom on a weekly basis makes communication to the level required to discuss reading regularly quite problematic, and those reluctant to read very often reply with a 'Dunno' grunt or 'I hate reading'. By using a reading dialogue journal we can get these students to open up a bit – eventually. In truth, teasing out key points in their reading to get a flavour of what they

---

5   T. M. Morretta and M. Ambrosini, *Practical Approaches for Teaching Reading and Writing in Middle Schools* (Newark, DE: International Reading Association, 2000).

understand can be painful, but it is hugely worthwhile. I tend not to concern myself too much with the technical aspects of writing here; that will come at some future point. Invite them in first and then, at some point, you will begin to see progress.

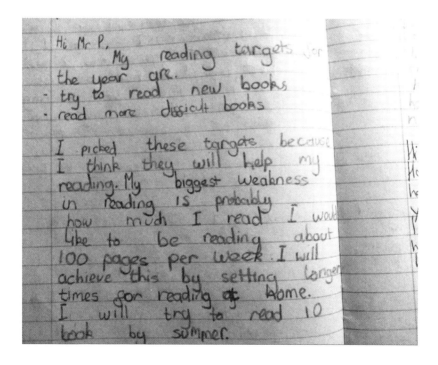

> another.
>
> I think that Meggie is most like me in this book, not only does she love books, but she has a strong personality. Unfavourably kind, but brave in more ways than one.
>
> This week, Mo, Meggie and Elinor escape from Capricorn's wrath. Dustfinger gets his hands on the keys, and they flee.

As I get to know their strengths and weaknesses, I can start adapting my questioning so they challenge and extend their reading skills, pushing them in directions they may otherwise not have considered. As a result, 99% of the pupils in my classes read and respond to reading very well every year; the other 1% are given the chance to begin the process of sharing their thoughts on reading. Theirs are often simplistic responses, but I *hope* a seed may have been planted that might grow in the years which follow.

The regular ten minute reading slots and the weekly journals give those students who 'don't like' reading the space to find out what is right for them. They can change books, hate books, drop books – as the famous quip goes,

'This is not a novel to be tossed aside lightly. It should be thrown with great force' – but they must read and respond to that reading in their journals. They will soon begin to see reading as something worth doing, as worth hanging in there for. And the journals look great on parents' evenings! They chart a child's reading development better than anything else I've encountered.

I've been using reading dialogue journals with my classes for years now. I started slowly with one class and the success I had with them led me to another, and another, and another. I don't use them with every single class but certainly they are appropriate for S1 and S2 (Years 8 and 9). There are thirty kids in each class, so the number of journals I need to deal with can add up to an unsurmountable pile – on occasion as many as sixty, sometimes more than this.

At times it can be impossible to do them justice, and many a Sunday I've been faced with a class set of journals needing to be dealt with and finding myself thinking that I could be using that time for other things. However, if I'm to really commit myself, and them, to this reading for pleasure thing, then this time needs to be my guarantee to them. You have to be convinced that the time spent is an investment that will pay off. If not, it will become an unwieldy chore.

I will respond to every student most of the time – I vow to respond at least once every two weeks, but as the year progresses I'll ask students to choose a journal partner and, with my help and advice, they respond to each other's journals. If you can make this work properly then it cuts down significantly on the workload. You can also set yourself a target of responding to the first half of your register one week, then the other half the next week. The others can get on with classwork and you've halved your weekly load!

On balance, I think the amazing things children pick up from reading, and the things they want to share with you, more than make up for the time it takes. When the journals are up and running, when the habit has kicked in and the routine is solid, the children have so much of value to say that it becomes a joy to read them. I love seeing my classes rushing in to see what I've written in their journals this week, eagerly engaging with the questions I want them to think about. And – hallelujah! – no book reviews.

Books Finished	Date finished	Books I plan to read
Breaking Dawn Twilight	1/09/10	
Remembrance	8/09/10	
The Kite rider	15/09/10	
Marked	7/10/10	Betrayed
Thirteen Pearls	20/10/10	Heidi
Heidi	9/11/10	Betrayed
Twilight	16/11/10	
New Moon	Can't remember date	Eclipse
Eclipse	Can't remember date	Breaking dawn
Breaking Dawn	Can't remember date	The Short Second life of Bree Tanner
Bree Tanner	31/12/10	Inkheart
Inkheart	2/2/11	Inkspell
Inkspell		Inkdeath

SO, HOW DO THEY WORK THEN?

Every child starts with the same three questions, written or pasted into the first page of their journals:

1   What is your book called and who wrote it?

2   Why did you choose it?

3   What has happened so far?

As the weeks pass, I respond individually to the direction each reader takes. In this way, I can participate in a dialogue with every student, asking them to think about certain areas and to clarify others. My responses usually take a three-question format: I ask them something about writer's craft, something about how the book relates to their own lives and, finally, I ask them to summarise this week's reading or to make a prediction (for example, 'What might happen to Skellig if Michael doesn't help him out of the shed? What would you do in this situation, and why?').

For the first question, I might ask them about the symbolism of the book's title or the development of a particular part of the plot. I might ask them about how the writer's use of imagery adds to the description of setting, or how the main character is introduced to the reader. For the second question, I'll ask about the relevance of the book's themes — for example, bullying, intolerance or family illness — and how (or if) that issue relates to the student's own life. I might ask them if the main character seems realistic or is like anyone they know ... even themselves. I might also ask if they've learned anything new or surprising from reading the book.

Usually, the final question I ask will be for them to summarise that week's reading in as few sentences as possible. Overall, I look for about half a page or so from some, less from more reluctant readers and writers. I can use their responses to gauge who is reading a book that is too simple or too difficult for them. I can also see whether they've understood symbolism, simile or characterisation, or whatever we've been studying that week.

Their journal offers the opportunity for quality interaction between me and every student about reading for pleasure. It provides reading and writing practice and an equal relationship between student and teacher which remains private. And while there's not an expectation that I will mark and correct written work, as that's probably a guarantee that reluctant readers will turn away from, I can pick up on habitual problems and address those within other classwork.

The students record the books they've read on a reading record pasted on the inside cover of their journals. Over the course of the year, the impact and sense of achievement can be impressive. Against their better judgement, and without realising it's happening, kids become readers. How did that happen?

Reading record

Books read	Date finished	Books I plan to read

THE ACCELERATED READER PROGRAMME

You now have in place a reading programme that, if adhered to consistently, will work very well for all your readers. It may take more effort than relying on a bought-in reading programme, but everyone will get more out of it and there will be long-term benefits. While it is not my intention to be purposely negative about Accelerated Reader (AR) or any other reading programme, well, I hope I've offered up a better alternative. AR, in particular, is widely used in UK schools and I'm aware that many teachers have their views on it. Of course, I can only speak from my own experience, but I've yet to be convinced by anything I've seen or heard about it.

While AR has been around since the late eighties, I first came across it about eight or nine years ago. It was an expensive buy-in so, of course, my school wanted it to work. Classes were set up and plans were made. All my younger classes (and one of my older, more challenging classes) would, once a week, read from a choice of books that were geared towards a specific reading level. My understanding is that if, after finishing a book, a student performed well at a short multiple choice test then they could advance to the next level. Certainly, if you looked through that little window in my class door you would have seen the children reading. And that's got to be a good thing, hasn't it?

But what I encountered wasn't good at all. The books seemed to be limited to those chosen by the company who ran AR. I could have created tests for specific books (I suppose), but that seemed like a whole lot of extra and unnecessary work. Students seemed to be discouraged from reading books that might have been too hard for them, and I hated that. When we become readers we dip into books haphazardly which give us a taste of things to come. AR seemed to actively discourage this. I also perceived, among the more reluctant readers, an eagerness to get to the end of their chosen books so they could get to the computer test. So I had classes full of readers, but no increase in a love of reading. Those who were already readers hated that their choices were so limited, and those who weren't gave up when there was no quiz at the end.

If you want your classes to be seen to be reading books then I'm sure this will get them doing just that. But what Kelly Gallagher observes in his book *Readicide* is right: 'Many teachers like Accelerated Reader and similar incentive-laden programs because they see students do a significant amount of reading. What they don't see is that programs such as AR and others that offer extrinsic rewards often lead to demotivating students after they have left the classroom.'[6]

I've mentioned AR very briefly during workshops I've led and noticed raised eyes and nods of agreement. My intention here is not to criticise teachers who use AR, but to suggest better ways of encouraging lifelong readers. In my view it is the relationship with a significant adult that is the best way of achieving this. If there is no one at home who does this, then it has to be you – their teacher.

---

6   Gallagher, *Readicide: How Schools Are Killing Reading and What You Can Do About It* p. 75.

Chapter 5
THE E-READER

While we decry the death of the book and the rise of the e-reader, you might imagine that the good old-fashioned book is being cast aside like your video recorder, your Walkman or those expensive notebooks that seemed a good idea at the time. That we can get more books on our phones than we can in our homes, more or less – unless you're the Queen – might suggest that the e-reader could be the greatest thing in publishing since Gutenberg. Possibly, but that's more likely to be Steve Guttenberg![1] I surprise myself when I remember that I'm on my second Kindle – the first one broke. I like to think it was my excessive use of the old thumbs as, at speed, I battered through *Madame Bovary* and countless other classics because they were free. It wasn't though; I sat on it. It doesn't matter much if you sit on a book.

Don't get me wrong. I did splash another £150 on a new one almost immediately because I like to have it on me when I'm out. I like reading it on the bus, in the pub or in Waterstones' cafe. I like having Bukowski's poetry alongside P. G. Wodehouse and the complete works of Shakespeare. All in my pocket. The problem is that it makes for a pretty stinky class library. A love of reading goes hand in hand with a love of books, and the libraries of our past, present and future become the wallpaper of our lives. As well as providing endless hours of entertainment, discovery, information and escapism, books have an aesthetic delight which our homes would be diminished without. So my Kindle is in my pocket, my bag or somewhere handy, but it's out of sight.

---

1   I thank you.

Owning a Kindle is very much like having a library in your pocket, and that's not necessarily a good thing for a reader. It's advertised as 'a dedicated e-reader'.[2] You can take it anywhere, just like a book, and carry as much reading material on it as you could never stock in your home (it's even got a real page turning facility, just like a book). However, when I find myself in a library or a bookshop I tend not to spend much of that time actually reading. Not since university have I really read in a library. Bookshops even less so. Like record shops, how can you stop in one place when there are so many potential nuggets in the goldmine? Like a bookshop, an e-reader is riddled with distractions.

If you're like me, then you've probably spent a lifetime building up your book collection. It takes up far too much space in your home, but it feels nostalgic and warming having it there. Kindle has changed my approach. I currently have about 500 books on it, half of them unread. I download free classics, so I have Dickens, Shakespeare, Aristotle, Tolstoy and many others. Never read them. Probably won't. I have poetry and prose, fiction and non-fiction, drama old and new. And here's the irony: the more I download, the less I read.

The books I have read, I never think of again. I can't see them, so I can't pick them up and flick through them, remembering characters fondly or rereading sections which made me laugh or cry. The visual pleasure of rows and rows of spines has been lost to me. Their colours, their order, their covers (by which you judge them) are what help us to build our reading histories. You can't lose a bookmark in the pages of a Kindle or fold over the corners or scribble a note. Being in a bookshop or a library twenty-four hours a day will lead you to distraction. Similarly, on a Kindle I spend my time reading the first page of ten books, never settling on one. When we use our e-readers we are faced with so many diversions that deep reading becomes impossible: the buttons are made to be pressed; the links invite you to follow them; there are built-in dictionaries, note takers and recommendations. All of these

2   See http://www.amazon.co.uk/gp/product/B00KDRUCJY/ref=sv_kinc_0.

add up to one hell of a temptation. And to find out why that was bad all along, we need to go back a few years to Ancient Greece and a wee fella by the name of Socrates.

SOCRATES

Of course, if it were up to Socrates we would never have begun reading at all.

The triumvirate of the Greek godfathers of the word – Socrates, Plato and Aristotle – helped pave the way to reading as we know it like no other group. But Socrates – or, for the purposes of this section, a moody and intimidating Marlon Brando – was so concerned with knowledge and the truth that he worried reading would give students the mistaken assumption that they had knowledge. But without discussion, questioning and thought, that so-called knowledge would be nothing but data. To him, the printed word was an impediment to learning and would lead to laziness and a gradual erosion of discussion and debate. So, without that discussion, books were merely a moment in time, untouched by any human hand beyond the writer's. Only that which the reader already knows can be affected by reading.

It was Socrates/Brando's assumption that books are frozen in time, that no interpretation is possible beyond the creator's and, in a bizarre historical echo of at least one 14-year-old student of mine *every single year*, he says: 'they [written words] seem to talk to you as though they were intelligent, but if you ask them anything about what they say, from a desire to be instructed, they go on telling you just the same thing forever'.[3]

---

3   Plato, *Phaedrus*, in *The Collected Dialogues of Plato*, ed. E. Hamilton and H. Cairns (Princeton, NJ: Princeton University Press, 1961), p. 521.

> It's just words. How am I supposed to know what the writer meant?
>
> S3 student in my school, every year

If Socrates turned up in my class with that poor attitude to his work I'd have to keep him behind for a quiet word. There are English teachers all over the world fighting for the premise that close reading (or reading comprehension) is fundamental to what we do in class. However, there is a point here: if we can link reading (and, more specifically, reading for pleasure) to the notion that all reading is linked to prior knowledge, then we begin to create readers.

Of course, at the finale of the first *Godfather* movie we see the end of the Brando era and the coronation of Al Pacino, determined to wipe out all opposition, to streamline and modernise operations. Unbeknownst to Socrates, Plato was quietly agreeing with everything his mentor said but, somewhat rebelliously, he was writing all of it down. When it was his turn to take the stage, he was less concerned about the stupefying effect of the written word – he actually agreed with Socrates that the printed word would spell the end of memory and of deeper knowledge – but, hell, he wrote everything down anyway. As Maryanne Wolf remarks, 'It is only because we can read the product of Plato's ambivalence that we can come to understand Socrates and the universal nature of his concerns.'[4]

Plato's respect for Socrates was clear, but he was caught in the contradictory trap of having one foot in each camp. He agreed that the written word was dangerous but he could not stop the onslaught of time and progress. If we'd listened to Socrates – who would later be charged by the citizens of Athens with the corruption of youth that many of us have faced in those oh so helpful end-of-year feedback forms we like to give children to create the illusion of voice – think of what might have happened. *Fifty Shades of Grey* may never have been written. Dan Brown would have had to get a real job.

---

4   Wolf, *Proust and the Squid*, pp. 219–220.

Having been mentored by Socrates, Plato, in turn, was mentor to Aristotle – the fella we should, perhaps, be thanking for giving us reading as a way of life. It has been argued that the Andy Garcia of our trio, Aristotle, is the godfather of the practice of private reading. While being clearly the weakest of the three in terms of intellectual weight, he was not as lightweight as we might think. (Go on, watch *The Godfather, Part III* again. You'll see.) The genie was definitely out of the bottle now. Aristotle was already immersed in a life of reading and understood that what we read can be added to our existing knowledge and passed on to future generations.

The kids in your class are no different, really. Of course, they have grown up in a different age, where being connected to their devices is as natural as buying comics was to older generations. Asking them to concentrate on one thing at a time is an even greater challenge. And if we struggle to cope with this, how can we expect them to?

THE INFORMATION SUPERHIGHWAY

The Internet, while being responsible for the end of reading as we know it – or so we might be told – takes our access to new information to ridiculous levels. What might be seen as the democratisation of knowledge should suggest a greater need for deeper reading so that we might sift through and judge that information. So how does this affect our quest for independent readers who read for pleasure? There is a danger that when children are faced with so much reading material, they skip over much of the text in order to get to the information they need, thus missing the detail. It's why we need to separate this type of reading from the immersive, joyful, lost-in-space reading experience of time spent with a good book.

Nicholas Carr observes that 'technology is just a tool, inert until we pick it up and inert once we set it aside again'.[5] A book is no different. It hides away an amazing story in its pages, waiting to be opened up and read. I regularly hold up a book in class and discuss the possibilities held within, the incredible worlds contained in that small package in my hand, before we get to reading it. Books can and do exist alongside technology.

We blame the Internet for our inability to concentrate on reading for any length of time, but perhaps we fail to comprehend that, in many ways, we are now far better at finding out what we need. Far from becoming poorer readers, we merely become different readers: our brains are adapting to the deluge of reading material being thrown at as. Rather than reading less, the online world allows us to become 'skilled hunters'[6] in search of what we need.

> Take your time, the books whispered to me in their dusty voices. We're not going anywhere.
>
> Nicholas Carr[7]

Reading for pleasure is not just about the words, it is about the experience: the weight of the book, the feel of the spine, the colours and images of the cover design. It is about the ability to flick through pages and feel the block on the left getting bigger and the block on the right getting smaller as you work your way through it. It is the joy of your first bookshelves and the adventure of filling them. It is staring admiringly at your growing set of Famous Fives, James Bonds or Harry Potters. It is about watching that reading life grow alongside you.

---

5   N. Carr, *The Shallows: How the Internet Is Changing the Way We Think, Read and Remember* (London: Atlantic Books, 2011), p. 53.

6   Joe O'Shea, quoted in Carr, *The Shallows*, p. 9.

7   Carr, *The Shallows*, p. 12.

When kids read books on their phones or e-readers (which I'm happy to let them do, by the way, they're reading: the novelty may wear off when they turn to a 'proper' book; let them be), it doesn't half seem like the death of something. Not to mention the constant niggle that every time they turn a page or scroll down you instantly think they're texting their mates. However, there are serious issues beyond a grumpy adult weeping over the death of their past. E-readers have become de rigueur in classrooms, just as they have in everyday life, but we should be aware of their drawbacks. A recent study recognised that, while tablet or Kindle readers developed similar levels of comprehension in terms of plot and character, paper readers recorded much higher levels of empathy and awareness of narrative coherence. It was also found that, when asked about the order of events in a book or to discuss context of events, then those who read on e-readers were significantly behind.[8]

When I read this article I did see the point. When I read on my Kindle I miss the opportunity to quickly look back at the opening chapter or reread a favourite part or one that needs clarification. I get depressed by the percentage in the corner quietly disapproving of my slow progress. Apparently, you can get thousands of books on the All-New Kindle E-Reader, but your book will never run out of batteries and you can turn the pages with a small child, anticipating the next pictures or words. Sorry Mr Kindle, but you just ain't cutting it.

However, while we should be wary of the effects of the e-reader on children's reading as 'almost everything about e-reading is preliminary and small scale at this point',[9] it might also be important to discuss any possible benefits.

8   See A. Flood, Readers absorb less on Kindles than on paper, study finds, *The Guardian* (19 August 2014). Available at: http://www.theguardian.com/books/2014/aug/19/readers-absorb-less-kindles-paper-study-plot-ereader-digitisation.

9   David Kleeman of research firm Dubit, quoted in S. Dredge, Are tablet computers harming our children's ability to read?, *The Guardian* (24 August 2015). Available at: https://www.theguardian.com/technology/2015/aug/24/tablets-apps-harm-help-children-read.

E-READERS IN THE CLASSROOM

There have been several experiments using e-readers in the classroom and these have come up with varying results.[10] I hasten to add that it isn't me who has done these experiments, but it would be remiss of me not to discuss the findings here. If you ever find yourself in the very fortunate position of having a whole class of children with e-readers, then you might like to take account of the following.

- One of the more popular uses of some e-readers is the text-to-speech function. For weaker or younger readers you can set the e-reader to read out the story (in an uncomfortably creepy voice) as the child reads along. There are clear benefits in word recognition and pronunciation to be had here. For visually impaired pupils it can be a necessity. But we also need to be aware that text-to-speech can become a permanent crutch if used excessively. We must ensure that it allows readers to develop their linguistic skills without becoming a replacement for the work required for them to become independent readers.

- The ability to increase text size can be hugely advantageous for inexperienced readers as well as for the visually impaired. Think of the times when you've been keen on reading certain books and have been put off by the ludicrously small font – hey, it comes to all of us eventually! Some of the classics you've never read become instantly more accessible on a Kindle. Think what that might mean for the more reluctant reader or those pupils with dyslexia who are put off by a full page of text.

---

10 See L. Gardener, A Kindle in the classroom: e-reading devices and reading habits, *Language Arts Journal of Michigan* 27(1) (fall 2011). Available at: https://core.ac.uk/download/pdf/10684690.pdf; and Princeton University, The E-reader Pilot at Princeton: Final Report (Executive Summary) (fall 2009). Available at: https://www.princeton.edu/ereaderpilot/eReaderFinalReportShort.pdf.

- If we are to encourage reading for pleasure as a life skill – something to be done outside school – then we must be prepared to trust our pupils and allow them to borrow e-readers for home use. Immediately this becomes a budgetary problem. Might we be creating a problem if we encourage the use of technology that they may not be able to access at home? The advantage of books in this situation is clear; if they stick a book in their bag and it gets lost or damaged, then replacement is a mere inconvenience. Expensive technology is a whole other ball game.

- One of the ways I've used a Kindle in the classroom is through the app. I often talk about the reading I'm doing, both at home and in school. When we discuss characters or settings, I often stick a paragraph from my current Kindle reading up on the whiteboard via the projector. I can point out sparkling sentences or great descriptions, examples of language that we've been studying or something that just takes my fancy which I'd like to share. It's a quick, clear and efficient way of capturing a teachable moment using my own reading for pleasure as the stimulus and the material.

> When you hold a book in your hands, you're in charge of the pace at which you read and images you choose to form.
>
> Jack Canfield and Gay Hendricks[11]

I've never really been convinced by the argument that the Internet has killed reading for kids. In reality, they do just as much reading, perhaps more, but in a different way. They skim and scan in more skilful ways than ever and they access more information than ever before. Where the problems come, I fear, is in our perception of the Internet as creating an attention deficiency – the inability to sit quietly and read for any length of time. If concentration spans

---

11   J. Canfield and G. Hendricks, *You've Got to Read This Book!* (New York: Harper Collins, 2007), p. xvii.

become eroded, we assume that reading long texts will become impossible for some.

And, in a way, that may be true. Our brains adapt to our environment and, as cognitive psychologist Susan Greenfield argues, our environment is changing at a rapid rate.[12] Is it any wonder that when overwhelmed with fast-paced titillation our brains are trying to adapt to many things happening at the one time, allowing for much less concentration time on any one thing? It's the old computer game argument. How can I stop and think when so many things are firing at me all at once? Greenfield suggests that selective attention – when we tune in to the things which grab our interest in short bursts – will trump the focused attention required to, for example, read a book. She describes a 2012 study involving 400 British teachers in which 'three-quarters reported a significant decline in attention spans'.[13]

It's hard to argue against, and perhaps emphasises the challenge of getting kids to read for pleasure. But it's an important challenge to overcome. When we become so immersed by the screens in front of our faces that we miss out on the real life-affirming experiences happening around us – think of the guy who misses the experience of hearing Bruce Springsteen and the E Street Band blasting out 'Born to Run' because he is too transfixed trying to film it on his phone and send it to his mates – then we must, perhaps, refocus.

However, maybe it's not so bad as we first suspect. Maybe reading shorter pieces of writing has its advantages. Developing into a good reader relies on the amount of background knowledge we have. When we have that background knowledge, we begin to make connections with new information, which is a lifelong process that builds and changes as we grow older. We're quick to judge young people who won't sit down and read *Pride and Prejudice*

---

12   S. Greenfield, *Mind Change: How Digital Technologies Are Leaving Their Mark On Our Brains* [Kindle edn] (London: Ebury, 2015).
13   Greenfield, *Mind Change*, loc. 497.

without getting bored. But we're quick to judge young people on anything, aren't we? Their eating habits, their fashion, their music, but, most especially, their reading habits. When was it exactly that we turned into our parents?

Ultimately, though, I just want them to read. If it turns out to be on an e-reader then so be it. The Kindle has clearly kindled an enthusiasm for reading. Book sales are going through the roof; whether those sales are paper or electronic is unclear and perhaps not important. Within a week in January 2015, two conflicting articles claimed that the sale of physical books had increased by 5% and also fallen by 'more than £150 million in five years'.[14] But take a walk around your local high street bookshop. It'll be busy with customers; it'll be crammed to the rafters with books new and old, shiny and tempting. There will be piles of D-list celebrity autobiographies flying out of the door as last minute Christmas gifts. Never to be read.

They're selling, though, in their millions. I can't imagine there has been a better time for young adult fiction. Whatever you think of the 'Harry Potter' books or the 'Twilight' series, they have spawned a generation of readers keen to get their hands on the next book in the series. But Marcus Sedgwick, Sophie McKenzie, Catherine MacPhail, Patrick Ness, David Almond, Kevin Brooke, Theresa Breslin, Celia Rees, Meg Rosoff and countless others are enthralling school kids all over the country today, yes today. They are marketed superbly but also written exquisitely.

So here's the thing. If you've got a classroom library full of duds – books you wouldn't touch with a big pole – bin them. Get some new ones. Charity shops are great. Ask those distant relatives who give you socks for Christmas to give you books instead, or at least vouchers. The aim is to brighten up the selection of books in your classroom. Make sure they are titles the pupils will want to pick and read, not something that's been there since books were invented.

---

14   See Trotman, Kindle sales have 'disappeared'; and Flood, Sales of printed books fall by more than £150m.

Chapter 6
TALKING ABOUT READING

The rise of the TeachMeet movement – I hesitate to call it an explosion as statistically only a very small percentage of teachers get involved – has confirmed the importance of enabling teachers to talk about their work. These partly informal gatherings have transformed the delivery of continuing professional development and allowed those in the classroom, previously left to suffer top-down, backside-numbing drearathons dressed up as professional development, some form of control over what they learn. And it's about the talk. The conversations we are now able to have with our colleagues allow us to articulate not only the frustrations of our teaching experiences, but also to develop thoughts and ideas about what we do and what we'd like to do.

English teachers like the sound of their own voices. We talk for a living. We talk about our work, the kids we teach, the stress of our lives. But we also love to talk about our reading. The reading communities in which we exist, whether formal or informal, are the result of years of reading and sharing our thoughts on reading. This becomes part of the experience of being a teacher and a way to articulate our musings, share intellectual concepts and find new books.

I recently rushed out to purchase the 'new' Harper Lee novel, *Go Set A Watchman*. Despite the negative press, I couldn't help it. I love *To Kill a Mockingbird* and teach it to at least every other year group. To dip back into the lives of Atticus and Scout was just far too tempting to turn down. However, when I finished it, smugly, sitting in the coffee shop in Waterstones in Glasgow, I immediately looked about for someone to talk to. There were about three other people reading it and I had to swallow the urge to yell 'Spoiler alert!'

I love talking about books. I want to question and be questioned. I want to have the same conversations about books that I have about TV, film and football. And I want that for the kids I teach too.

Developing that kind of culture in classrooms is an essential part of the reading experience for young people. Having worked so hard to get them reading, and begin the process of allowing them to develop a reading habit in their lives, now is the time to open them up to the views of others and to encourage them to share. It isn't enough that they read. They need opportunities to bring their books to life through talk, debate and discussion. They also need to hear what their peers are reading. There is no greater book recommendation than from a friend, so tapping in to that classroom of potential book reviews is really powerful. Coming up with useful and fun strategies for them to do that is what this chapter is about.

BOOK SPEED-DATING

There is an expectant hush as the class enter to a strange desk arrangement. They giggle excitedly as they sit in rows, fifteen in a line facing another fifteen. The room is not normally set out like this, so the teacher is clearly up to something. Their hesitancy as they take their seats sets them on edge. Is this an opportunity to sit with my mates? Of course it is. It always is. At the far end of the row of chairs then, away from the teacher's desk? Don't mind if I do. This should be a laugh!

They don't know what's about to hit them.

Book speed-dating throws kids. They don't quite know what to make of it. I ask them, very quickly, to think about how they might 'sell' the book they are currently reading to others. Not an easy task, but they usually scratch something together. On the first bell – a miniature hand-held bell I stole from a board game at some point – the fifteen on the left start talking about their books. They summarise, they sell and they repeat. After thirty seconds, I ring the bell again. The group opposite start up. Talking and talking.

The room is buzzing with noise and it's all great fun. After another thirty seconds I ring the bell again. The group on the left move along one seat. The one sitting at the back comes to the front. Bell. Go again. The fifteen on the left repeat their thirty second sales pitch. Perhaps slightly more confidently this time, slightly more assured and focused. They get better at it each time they do it. The room seems to get noisier after each ring of the bell as they begin to relax and enjoy themselves, starting to understand the rules. They are moving, talking, having fun.

By the time they've been all the way round and returned to their original partners, fifteen minutes have passed. They have repeated their talks fifteen times. They have heard another fifteen short book talks. I give them a wee heart-shaped sticky note and ask them to go and find the book they fancy the most. This provides a few more minutes of chatter about books, reminders and confirmations. We leave the sticky notes on the board for a day or two so they can check out other students' choices, as can other classes. They leave the room talking about books. The next time we go to the library, they take their sticky notes with them.

Book speed-dating is great fun, but it also allows you to nurture several skills: the nature of multiple talks ensures that your pupils are learning to summarise properly and make decisions about what is most important; they hear fifteen other reviews, so they can no longer ever employ the excuse that they 'don't know any good books'; they may well be fulfilling any assessment for talk outcomes you have to cover; but, most importantly, you are embedding a culture where books are something we share and enjoy and have fun with.

BOOK GROUPS

I'll be honest and admit that I've never been part of a book group. I've never wanted to, never considered it, don't plan to. Perhaps I'm too opinionated to consider the views of others, especially when it comes to a book I have strong opinions on. It might well be a great way to develop a reading culture across the school – among pupils and staff – but I'd be a hypocrite if I promoted it as something you should have a go at as I haven't done it myself. I do, however, recommend expanding your reading boundaries to other departments.

Teachers are highly intelligent, university educated professionals and are usually voracious readers who often want to discuss their reading with others. Creating a reading culture beyond the English department is a really important way to reinforce the message that reading is an important life skill. We've had displays of photographs of teachers reading in my school, many in bizarre poses, and teachers are encouraged to talk to pupils about the books they're reading.

What greater resource do we have than teachers from all subject areas talking about their own reading and modelling the reading life? It ain't just English teachers who need to bang on about reading: teachers of other subjects encouraging their pupils to read subject related texts out of school is immensely powerful too. Teachers reading out interesting passages from books they've read and spending just a few minutes discussing the implications of the text can be transformative. Pupils begin to see reading models all around the school: this reading thing is something that all clever adults do, not just geeky English teachers.

BOOK CONFERRING

Those kids who don't have books at home, who don't see adults reading at home and don't ever think of reading at home also lack someone to talk to about books. They often don't know where to turn when they read something good or where to look for their next book, so it's important that we plug that gap ourselves. We need to talk to them about their reading. So, please stop sending kids to the library unaccompanied. It's not at all like throwing them into the swimming pool without a rubber ring. They may well learn to swim that way – or they may scream for their mums as I did all those years ago. (I still can't swim; being thrown in didn't help.) Faced with walls of books is no way to develop readers. They have no means of distinguishing between the good and the bad beyond the front covers.

This is why your more reluctant readers will often opt for bland movie adaptations or totally inappropriate 700-page doorstoppers. They don't have a clue. But when we talk about our own reading and ask them about theirs, we are providing a source of information previously unavailable to them. As a teacher, I can begin to comprehend just how much they understood about that last book and guide them towards another one I think they may enjoy. As a reader, I can share my experiences with good books: the times I laugh, cry and want to scream while reading. Participation in a fully literate reading community necessitates the ability and the willingness to talk about what we read.

Allowing your pupils to talk to each other about their reading is a fantastic way of developing that culture. I call this 'book conferring'. You needn't spend too much time on this – perhaps five minutes to share their thoughts on their book so far, or you could give them a specific focus, such as character, setting, major incident or problem. Circulate as they are talking but don't butt in. If there are any students who aren't participating, find out why, but don't discipline them; instead, promote the positive and praise those who have done well by asking them to share their interesting observations with the class.

You could also ask them to complete sixty second book talks. Once a week I invite five pupils to prepare a very short talk, which could be a 'My next book' feature. No spoilers, but a promotion of the book and why someone might want to read it next. This is quick and is great fun too.

All of these strategies can help, but there is nothing more effective than quietly sidling up to pupils in class or in the library and gently asking them about their books. During our ten minute reading sessions at the beginning of lessons, I lift my eyes from my own book secretly and try to catch someone smiling or laughing or looking particularly engrossed in their books. I make a point of catching up with that pupil during the lesson and finding out what was happening. Get in there while it's still fresh in their minds. They'll be delighted you did so!

PODCASTING

When I was a spotty teenager at school, I had to record a speech for a class project we were doing on *Macbeth*. It took the form of a chat show-type structure and about five of us crowded around a tape recorder which, according to my diminishingly effective memory, took up half the room. Once we had finished giggling our way through the whole performance, we took the eight-reel tape back to the teacher, where it was put into a cupboard, never ever to be seen again. Box ticked. Project completed. Nothing learned.

Thankfully, technological advances mean that we no longer give up quite so much space to gadgets in the classroom and we can design tasks that are useful and worthwhile. For those students who find speaking up in class difficult, recording their thoughts is a clever way to allow them to share their reading. Podcasting isn't a new idea, but you can use it to assess reading, talking and listening. You can send your pupils into a corner of the library or the classroom, or you can ask them to record at home, which they may do more comfortably and confidently. The podcasts can be quickly erased and improved upon and, unlike writing, they don't need to be absolutely perfect. Your sixty second book talks would work perfectly on a podcast, and can be collected and shared as a comprehensive guide to fiction for school kids. Podcasts can be given as homework tasks or encouraged as something to be completed after finishing any book.

All you need is a smartphone. There are several apps you can use – Easy Voice Recorder, Opinion Podcasts and Mobile Podcaster might be good places to start – and the large multinational fruit-based company's phone even has a voice recorder built in. Your pupils may have smartphones in their pockets already or you can lend them yours. You can also buy some neat little recorders for the classroom that don't cost too much. They are simple to use and (this is so helpful) your pupils can very easily e-mail the files to you once they have completed them. In the past, I've had a class blog where I could assemble the podcasts, so pupils who are struggling to find a book can be directed towards their peers talking about books they've read. Over the years, you can keep adding to the set and organise them into different sections, genres and year groups.

And, of course, if anybody 'important' comes a-calling, you have evidence of learning in spades. You can also send them home to parents and even get them to assist in creating the podcasts. There are loads of websites available to help with the creation of more polished podcasting (www.podomatic. com is one of my favourites). Your kids can create a series of podcasts on reading (or anything else for that matter), and these provide a modern and creative way to display their learning. More importantly, they are developing and sharing their reading histories, thereby adding to their skills and strategies.

BOOK TALKS

Nancie Atwell, the 2015 World Teacher of the Year (whatever that means), makes book talks a structured part of her classroom.[1] She teaches primary

---

1   N. Atwell, *In the Middle: New Understandings About Writing, Reading, and Learning*, 2nd edn (Portsmouth, NH: Heinemann, 1998), p. 37.

age children, so perhaps this would work better with younger kids, but she models the talks and spends time discussing the books she has read. The talks become a weekly event and, over time, the children take over and prepare talks on their own reading. Like podcasts, book talks need only last a minute or so, but you can see the potential to expand the book knowledge of both talker and listener.

'It isn't enough to fill a classroom with great titles,' says Atwell. 'An important role of the reading teacher – the most important work, according to my students – is to become so intimate with good books that we bring life, with our voices, to the tattered spines that line the shelves of our libraries.'[2] I love the idea of bringing books to life 'with our voices' because it takes us all the way back to Socrates and his belief that we learn through talk. We develop readers by creating a community in which they feel comfortable enough to share not only what they've read, but also how that reading has affected them.

It's important that the book talks are brief and pretty much straight to the point: 'Why should you read this book? Well, here's why ...' No one wants to listen to a long plot summary, and your students may not be comfortable with being the centre of attention for too long. There are very obvious literacy lessons to be had here – persuasive language for one – but try to keep them as informal as possible. The last thing you want to do is turn kids off reading by insisting on language work on top of everything else. Like any good review, though, we should encourage them to hint at something amazing, something to look forward to, some reason to get to the end of *this* book. Get them to finish with a question. Leave their readers hanging. Leave their readers desperate to grab that book out of the hands of the reviewer. Why wouldn't you?

---

2   N. Atwell, *The Reading Zone: How to Help Kids Become Skilled, Passionate, Habitual, Critical Readers* (New York: Scholastic, 2007), p. 67.

Over time, these book talks take care of themselves, with very little input from teacher. Don't stop talking to the children informally on a daily basis though. Like their reading journals, you can develop a conversation with the readers in your class as they make their way through increasingly challenging books, making recommendations and asking questions along the way.

CLASS CULTURE

Of course, part of being a reader is being able to dismiss books as being rotten or rubbish. We don't want to create a climate where kids are given the message that criticising books isn't allowed. One of Daniel Pennac's 'Rights of the Reader' is 'the right not to finish a book'.[3] I do this regularly: I have just quit Tim Winton's *Cloudstreet* halfway through. (I couldn't abide David Mitchell's *Cloud Atlas* either. Is it a cloud thing? Maybe. *Frantically googles more cloud books to give up on.*) Like anything else, becoming a fussy, opinionated reading bore is part of the whole package.

Talking about books teaches kids, who may feel pressurised into finishing a book they've chosen from the library which they don't like, that it takes time to find a book that fits them. And it's okay to dismiss five before they get to the one for them. I tell them that they wouldn't give up on chocolate because they didn't like a Mars bar. They'd try a Twix, a Ripple, a Curly Wurly even; they'd try everything in the shop first. Choosing a book should be no different. No wonder they develop negative experiences of reading if they're told what they must read.

As long as they can articulate why they don't like a book – they couldn't relate to the characters, the plot seemed far-fetched, the vocabulary was too

---

3   Pennac, *The Rights of the Reader*, right number 3.

challenging – then it is perfectly okay to shelve it. What a book talk should do, however, is try to accentuate the positive through the reader's enthusiasm. That's what will begin to engage their peers and encourage them to get stuck in. Think of each talk as a sales pitch – and promote them as such – because we want to collate as many positive experiences as possible.

Everything I've argued for so far in this book has been about developing readers in a culture where reading is valued and respected. Without dipping too far into the depths of cultural capital, the ability and willingness to talk about our reading and to take part in literate conversations about books is an important part of that. How will they be able to get outraged at *The Guardian* letters page without it? However, as part of your everyday practice in the classroom, and alongside many of the strategies I've written about so far, there is a very good chance you have already been creating that reading culture you have wanted. Now we've talked about talking, let's ramp it up a little and talk about writing about reading. Are you still listening?

Chapter 7
WRITING ABOUT READING

Okay, cards on the table … I'm going to say that I've never been quite convinced by the argument that being a good reader makes you a good writer. And, yes, I've read all the advice from great writers who say that to be a better writer you must read. Of course you must. However, the correlation which might suggest that one naturally leads to the other seems flawed to me. And a little bit lazy. I've tried to argue the case for reading up until now, but both reading and writing are highly complex skills and to link them together so casually might be mistaken and even damaging for some kids.

But we throw the line around quite freely, to the pupils themselves and to their parents: read more and your writing will improve. Guaranteed. But it's not as simple as that, is it? What we may be doing is creating even more barriers for some. The expectation that, having helped develop a class full of readers, you will inevitably have a class full of writers is, I think, an error. That's why we have committed, regular readers in our classes who can struggle to accurately convey their thoughts on a piece of paper. That's why we create greater problems for some kids when we ask them to write lengthy book reviews immediately after they've finished reading.

Undoubtedly, reading helps with many things. Chiefly, it allows us to broaden our knowledge of the world and our understanding of increasingly sophisticated vocabulary, but that doesn't necessarily transfer to the page when it comes to writing. The best writers in my class are always great readers, no doubt about that; but there are those who are perhaps reluctant readers, the ones we've been discussing in the six chapters so far, who often struggle with writing; and there can be voracious readers who struggle too. We make a direct causal link between the skills of reading and the skills of writing at our peril: we can turn kids away from reading even more by asking them to write about it without proper planning and thought.

Perhaps it's because writing is a more demanding discipline to both teach and learn. We may be able to hide our inability to read well, but we can't do that with writing. It is there on the page for all to see. Praising students is all very well; placing their work prominently on the 'Good work' noticeboard is all very well; but kids know instantly when their writing isn't as good as their mate's. The physicality of holding a pencil and creating shapes on the page can be a real challenge to those who haven't learned how to do it properly. For those who hold their pencils with a strange grip, rather than the comfortable manner that you and I adopt, each writing task is a tough challenge, potentially humiliating and certainly not one to throw about lightly when we connect it to reading for pleasure.

Gary Wilson argues that for some boys, the development of motor skills comes much later, so asking them to write can be a painful experience – quite literally.[1] Because of this, they struggle to present their work in a way in which they take pleasure and it becomes an embarrassment – an embarrassment that many may never get over. Regardless of how much we praise their ideas and understanding, their writing is a very public announcement of their failure. If it looks bad, they know it looks bad, and no amount of praise about the use of adjectives or punctuation will convince them otherwise, particularly when sitting alongside the beautifully produced work of other students.

We do a lot of writing in the English classroom. Of course we do. And linking reading for pleasure with writing about reading for pleasure seems such a

---

1   G. Wilson, *Breaking Through Barriers to Boys' Achievement: Developing a Caring Masculinity*, 2nd edn (London: Bloomsbury, 2013), p. 18.

natural fit. You've read a book? Great. Tell me all about it. How? Well, funny you should ask ...

THE HORROR OF THE BOOK REVIEW

There's a special small corner of hell reserved for the lengthy classroom book review, and next to it sit the teachers who have set them as tasks. We've all set them: I did in my early years of teaching. We all had to do them at school ourselves, so why not force our students to do them? You give all that time over to personal reading, so there has to be a payback.

Well, no, not necessarily. Is time really such a luxury that we need to justify the space we turn over to reading with some form of quantifiable forced assessment at the end? And if we are really encouraging kids to read for pleasure, have we thought through the reasons for asking them to write a book review, or the damage to our initial intent that it might have done?

In my first few years of teaching I asked my classes to write book reviews as a standard task. Perhaps I saw it as a way of checking their understanding of the books they read. Perhaps I saw it as an opportunity for them to write about a book of their choice. Perhaps I saw it as a way of replicating what I had to go through and what every English teacher, seemingly, had to do at school. Whatever the reason, I was wrong! Despite the odd gem from the kids who were already skilled readers and writers, the whole process usually ended up with a collection of poorly thought out nonsense, homework referrals and steely resistance from some to ever read another book while they were in my class. And the marking load. Oh my god! The marking load.

Weak readers often tend to be weak writers. As we've seen, it can be a difficult task to get kids back into books after some poor early experiences and to do so takes time, patience, empathy, gentleness and focused support. I try to be very careful not to completely turn them off reading at this point. As adults, unless we are addicted to www.goodreads.com, we wouldn't ever think of writing a review of a book we'd read – not unless we were paid to do so, especially a book that we'd chosen to read for pleasure. By asking kids to do this you are pushing reading for pleasure into a bag that contains all sorts of other issues, ensuring that both become a chore.

What is it we intend to achieve by setting a book review as a writing task? To allow our pupils to express their thoughts and develop their ideas on books they have read? Quite possibly. Is it to check for understanding, to check that they are genuinely reading or to check that the books they read were appropriately demanding? Possibly. What can tend to happen, however, is that the whole exercise becomes a test of writing rather than reading, leaving the reluctant reader/writer with a reminder that both are challenging and to be avoided.

Of course, it would be a shame not to allow for reader responses in class. You should, however, consider your reasons for asking for those responses and what you will eventually do with them. You've encouraged them to read; they've finished that book you found for them. Now what?

WAIT A MINUTE, MR POSTERMAN!

Strangely, for a boy growing up just outside Glasgow, I had a wee childhood love of Liverpool Football Club. I had no affiliation with Liverpool; perhaps I'd seen them on TV winning lots of games in the late seventies, once they had signed Kenny Dalglish – Scotland's best player at the time (or of all time). I was given a huge poster of Dalglish in his new Liverpool kit and it looked fabulous on my bedroom wall. Over the next few years, I would add to that one until all four walls and the ceiling were covered in posters of Liverpool players, teams and memorabilia. After a while, the wonderful Dalglish poster which started it was lost in a sea of colours and inferior players. Eventually I took them all down when I grew up and discovered Debbie Harry.

The classroom poster is similar, whether it's created by the pupils or it's something you've picked up at a local bookshop, on holiday or purchased from Amazon. They look lovely when they go up. Soon enough, though, the intended purpose is lost and it becomes mere wallpaper. Early on in my teaching career, I would ask kids to create a poster related to their books, describing some aspect of the novel they found most appealing. They were sometimes clever, mostly not. They went up on the wall and filled a space for a while. Then they got 'Dalglished' and disappeared. No one read them, then they would peel and fade ...

If you'd like your pupils to respond to their reading in some form – not necessarily for assessment purposes but to allow them to express their views on what they've read – then I'm not sure creating a poster is the right way to go about it. On the one hand, posters can be 'masterpieces of design' and communicate 'a simple idea as efficiently as possible with the maximum economy of language'.[2] On the other hand, they can be a massive waste of a pupil's time, dreadfully planned and executed and a completely wasted lesson in which no one learns anything whatsoever.

They are masterpieces of design. They communicate a simple idea as efficiently as possible with the maximum economy of language. As such, maybe they are worthy of study in art or design; maybe historians do need to look at propaganda posters; maybe it's worthwhile for geographers to look at tourism posters. Maybe.

---

2   D. Didau, A heck of a lot of posters, *The Learning Spy* (20 September 2015). Available at: http://www.learningspy.co.uk/featured/posters/.

Hywel Roberts claims that 'Display is a reflection of you. What do your walls say about you?'[3] So, a whole series of poorly planned, hastily completed book posters is sending out entirely the wrong message: 'I don't think things through'. I'd be wary of saying that posters are completely useless; clearly they have some purpose in certain contexts. But if I'm going to spend class time working on them, I want to be absolutely sure what that purpose is. If your class are creating book posters, make sure they are of a high standard and ensure they are regularly updated. Use them as a recommendation space which is forever changing. Don't create imaginary film posters or new front covers; create back covers with original blurbs. Have one or two carefully chosen quotations, not a whole load of them.

And *use* them. Refer to them if a child is searching for a book to read. But don't overdo them. I rarely think of Kenny Dalglish now. Debbie Harry, on the other hand ...

BOOK TWEETS

Besides, there are other more meaningful and constructive ways with which you can encourage the students to share thoughts on their reading.

That sentence was written in 140 characters. Exactly. Go on, count them if you want, but I assure you there are exactly 140 characters. I was very particular because this section is all about Twitter. Or book tweets to be precise. If you're unaware of Twitter (and where have you been?), it is a social media site which takes up too much of your valuable time and usually ends up with someone getting upset over some imagined slur. It limits messages to exactly 140 characters. So if you're looking for a reason to avoid that pile of

---

3   H. Roberts, *Oops! Helping Children Learn Accidentally* (Carmarthen: Independent Thinking Press, 2012), p. 136.

marking, then Twitter is the fella for you. It's proving quite popular among teachers these days. In fact, it is unlikely that this book would ever have been written if it hadn't been for the connections I've made through Twitter.

When it comes to reading for pleasure – not the study of literature but a choice of books to be read independently – book tweets are brilliant. They are exactly that: book reports in 140 characters.

There are rules:

- The title and author must not be used. It's Twitter. Why waste valuable characters when you could write this at the bottom of your tweet?

- Tweets must be grammatically perfect and punctuated properly. No abbreviations and no text speak.

- They must be as close to 140 characters as possible. No escape routes.

Younger student groups love and are infuriated by them in equal measure. They don't always find it easy, but they do manage to condense what they love about the books they have read into short tweets. And isn't that worth it, pupils reflecting on their reading in a shorter, snappier and more memorable way than the lengthy review? (They also make great wall displays that can serve as a book recommendation wall.)

This is not a substitute for real responses to literature. We still study challenging texts and respond in lengthy essays as part of the course, but the time saved from marking meaningless, grudgingly written, dull, monotonous book reports can be used for good old-fashioned reading time; and that's the *only* way to encourage young people to read.

Book tweets create a buzz about reading in the classroom. They are quick, short, snappy and fun, and they genuinely encourage an enjoyment of reading in any subject. Why not use them for quick-fire revision notes? Everyone in class takes a different point and writes a tweet. It could work ... And not a computer or techy tool in sight.

Check out these examples from an S1/Year 8 class:

- *Storm Catchers* by Tim Bowler – Fraser

  When Ella gets captured during the storm, the family also find out a bit more about their own past. More than they wanted to ...

- *Sleepwalking* by Nicola Morgan – Rebecca

  People are programmed at birth to not have emotions like rage, sorrow, etc. Some go wrong, called Outsiders. Really interesting and weird.

- *The Knife of Never Letting Go* by Patrick Ness – Megan

  Todd is the only almost-man in Prentiss town. A place where everyone can hear everyone else's thoughts. He finds a spot of complete silence.

- *Journey to the River Sea* by Eva Ibbotson – Danielle

  Maia, an orphan, is about to start a new life in the Amazon rainforest. But did Maia know what was ahead of her? This book is funny and true.

You see? Easy.

BLOGGING

Twitter and social media have made writers of us all. We are communicating in writing more than ever before. Judging the quality of that communication, well, I'll leave up to you … But access to information and opportunities to write have never been more available. I wouldn't be sitting here tapping away right now if it weren't for blogging. On 1 January 2011, I clicked 'publish' and a new life began. I've written hundreds of posts, some rubbish, some I'm proud of; but I shared and wrote and shared and wrote. This blogging can be something special. So how can we tap in to this in our classrooms?

Blogging in the classroom is not a difficult thing to do, and it's reasonably simple to set up. Access to tech can be the problem, particularly finding enough computers to get a class of thirty all logged on at the same time. However, once they're up and running they can (more or less) manage it themselves: in their own time, at home, at lunchtime. So it's worth investing a little bit of time in getting it right at the beginning. You can create networks only accessible in the classroom or between class members. You can decide whether blogs are to be shared in school, out of school, whether they're to be public or private. Depending on your class, some kids will be quite happy to share and comment on each other's work, while some may need some time to gain confidence.

You can get kids blogging about their reading on a regular basis. Like the reading dialogue journals I mentioned in Chapter 4, you could interact in a weekly post where readers share their thoughts on that week's reading. You could also nominate a student to blog for that week and have every other student comment on their work. Be careful with that one though – it takes time to build trust.

Blogs enable you to create portfolios of student work and allow parents to interact with it if they choose. There are obvious implications here as some parents have no access to such technology, but if you can get it right (for some at least) then it can reap amazing benefits in and out of the classroom.

I set up a 'Bookworm Blog' with an S1 class (Year 8) and had the class spend the year posting 100 word book reviews. They had to be exactly 100 words long (not 99, not 101) and could not use the title or author. They were also banned from using certain words and expressions – such as: 'A book I have read …' and 'My favourite part of the novel was …' – and attention to detail was the key. Perfect spelling, perfect punctuation, sophisticated vocabulary; there was a clear literacy focus. The task was not overly onerous for reluctant writers, and talented writers could get stuck in to their thesauruses and find some blinding vocabulary.

The best part though is the permanence of these reviews. I can use them with subsequent classes, directing them to great responses from their peers. The essential factor in writing about reading for pleasure is creating an audience for whom the reviews will have meaning.

SO, WRITING ABOUT READING?

It would be a shame to miss out on opportunities for students to respond to their reading, and it stands to reason that some form of writing about the reading they do for pleasure might be a healthy addition to a child's education and to the work of the class. I've tried to suggest that there are ways in which those responses don't need to be 'busy' work and can enhance the reading culture you have created. You really want to tap in to their conversations, so take time to embed some of these strategies into your approach to promoting reading for pleasure.

Once they begin to develop that reading habit, your students will have much to say about their books, and we should give them the channels to share what they think and develop their abilities to do so. That is, of course, part of a reading life. Writing about reading is not an optional extra. It is a fundamental part of the process in promoting reading for pleasure. You'll want your guys to know exactly why they're writing what they're writing; you'll want them to automatically turn to their reading dialogue journals when they're ready to do so. And they will only do that if they see the value and the benefit.

Writing about reading works because it creates a natural audience for the work. Their journal becomes a conversation which informs both teacher and student of progress, difficulty and enjoyment. Their book tweets become short, sharp book reviews – a genuine advertisement, one which both 'publicises' and informs future readers of its worth – which, like Twitter itself, is being constantly refreshed with new material. They become bloggers, creating online reference points and collating their thoughts on reading. As an occasional blogger, especially about reading, I've found that having the space to write down my ideas not only helps me to clarify my thoughts but it can also provide a forum within which I can share my confusion. When children write about their reading, with a focused end point, it allows them to do the same.

SEVEN CHAPTERS IN …

All of the strategies I've described so far have, at different times, worked very well in my classroom. Not all of them work with every class I've taught, but there are a wide variety of things from which to choose. But it would be crazy to attempt everything at once. You'd never get anything done and, if you are a full-time English teacher in a large secondary school, you wouldn't survive a term.

But we started on the assumption that kids are often reluctant readers and, if you've got to this point in implementing some of the ideas in this book, then hopefully you've got them reading and enjoying that reading. Good on you. However, we now need to consider what happens when we are not there for them. Will they read if we take away the space and the encouragement we provide daily? Have they yet turned their reading into habit?

Chapter 8
THE READING HABIT

I was in Nashville, Tennessee, and after the show I went to a waffle house. I'm not proud of it, but I was hungry. And I'm sitting there eating and reading a book. I don't know anybody, I'm alone, so I'm reading a book. The waitress comes over to me like, [*gum smacking*] 'What'chu readin' for?' I had never been asked that. Not 'What am I *reading*?', but 'What am I reading *for*?' Well, I guess I read for a lot of reasons, but it's basically so I don't become a ******** waffle waitress.

Bill Hicks[1]

It turns out that changing our habits is hugely problematic. The end of the sofa you sit on, the side of the bed you sleep on, the glass of wine you have on a Friday night, the cigarette. Our bodies become conditioned to do things compulsively and automatically. Charles Duhigg, in his fascinating book *The Power of Habit*, comes to the conclusion that change is much harder than we think: 'We know that a habit cannot be eradicated – it must, instead, be replaced.'[2] This raises difficulties when attempting to encourage reading for pleasure as a habit: when reading is something you do, not something that is an effort; when the question is, 'What are you reading?' not 'Are you reading?'

---

1   B. Hicks, *Love All the People: Letters, Lyrics, Routines* (London: Constable & Robinson, 2005), p. 19.
2   C. Duhigg, *The Power of Habit: Why We Do What We Do and How to Change* (London: Heinemann, 2012), p. 92.

Duhigg recognises that the power of habit is developed from three key steps: cue, routine, reward. The cue is whatever signals the habit: a craving, an urge for a biscuit, the time of day you normally crack open a bottle of beer. There is neither rhyme nor reason to this – you've simply always done it: 'Habits emerge because the brain is constantly looking for ways to save effort.'[3] It is easier and, in the short term, more pleasurable to do what we've always done. We like to be lazy at times, clicking away at the remote, feet up.

The routine is the action – drinking the wine, eating the chocolate, switching on the TV; the familiar routine that involves little effort and makes us feel safe. They are embedded by repetition. They are what we do and, like driving or deleting spam e-mails, we do them without thinking.

The reward is the feeling you have afterwards: the sugar rush, the slightly cloudy wine head, the relaxation. We want something good at the end of this routine. But we have to be convinced that the reward is worthwhile if we are to embed changes.

To alter bad habits, Duhigg suggests that we need to change the cue to something more positive. We might leave our running shoes beside the bed or by the door as a reminder. We need to force ourselves to change the routine. The reward comes from the feeling of doing something much more beneficial.

Embedding reading habits in young children is an even greater challenge. How do we do that *and* turn kids into readers who know exactly 'what they're reading *for*'?

---

3   Duhigg, *The Power of Habit*, p. 17.

FEEDING THE HABIT

I don't need much of a cue to read. I'm already there: on the bus, in the car, in the pub before the football. My wife laughs at me because I can wake up at any time during the night and immediately pick up my book, tired or not. Creating such a habit in your students requires you to develop a cue that they can recognise (even if they fight against it for a while). It needs to be something they expect, which happens every time and which allows them the freedom to act by themselves.

The cue in my class is entering the classroom. All of my classes start with ten minutes of reading (see Chapter 2) and they know how it works. I welcome them to the class and walk to my computer where I start a ten minute countdown. By the time I get to my seat, they have their books out and are reading.

As they respond to that cue, the reading routine kicks in. To begin with you'll need to keep an eye on the ones who are easily distracted – habits don't grow without being nurtured, y'know. I read my book while they read theirs, raising an eyebrow now and then, perhaps catching the attention of miscreants who get back to their books. Those who have finished their book at home the night before, or who have forgotten their book, should have a cue close by. They reach for their reading dialogue journals and scribble down some thoughts about their reading for that week. No one is allowed to opt out. No one gets on with other class work. This is our reading time and we take it seriously. Over time, your room will develop a lovely oasis of calm during your crazy, busy day.

The real difficulty is in convincing the kids that there is a reward worth striving for here. Why read? The long-term benefits are unquestionable, but telling a 13-year-old that in about ten years' time they'll thank me seems a bit of a hollow message. I repeat that message constantly, but in the short term they will finish books, some for the very first time on their own, and their responses can be reward enough. When you create a buzz about books, the reward might be to have a go at a shiny new book in your class library. Over time they will see the benefit. Their confidence in reading more challenging books will grow; their reluctance to go anywhere near a book will fizzle away.

The power of this reading habit takes longer to hit for some than for others, but as their teacher you need to stick to this rigid routine. Every lesson. No exceptions. You need to persist with the message even when it seems as though you're battering your head against a brick wall. Focus on the ones who will love ten quiet minutes to read. Play the class numbers game. I tell student teachers that, in general, one third of any new class will be on your side, one third will be against you and the other third will be undecided. Get the ambivalent ones to sway towards you and the rest – mostly – will follow. Over time, the ten minutes at the beginning of your lesson will start to work like clockwork.

A READING PERIOD – SERIOUSLY?

My hair is going grey, I'm slowing down and a strange thing has begun to happen to me: on more occasions than I'd care to admit, and totally out of character I hasten to add, I've begun shedding a tear or two on seeing emotional things on TV. Usually sporting occasions, but the odd time on the nightly news, a sad movie or a stray Tom Waits lyric. What is happening to me? 'What is this salty discharge?'[4]

But what really makes me want to weep in school is the realisation that some kids still have a 'reading period'. Once a week. That's it. Oh, come on …

---

4   'The Serenity Now', episode 3 (season 9), *Seinfeld*, dir. A. Ackerman (originally aired 9 October 1997).

Whoever became a reader in circumstances like these? The only encouragement given by your teacher is a forty minute session, with no interaction, no opportunity to share books and opinions, knowing that you won't have to do it again for another week. Because it's not important to the teacher, is it? There are other things to do: reading for pleasure doesn't have a grade, as such, so it can always slip off the table, for this week anyway. Very often reading periods are irregular, unannounced, 'let's read today' sessions when planning has taken a back seat. Unfair of me? Perhaps, but probably not.

Of course we have lots to cover during the school year. But a reading period is probably as bad as none at all, possibly worse. The message going out to the children is that this is all the time they are getting for reading, and if they want to do more then it's up to them – 'in your own time'. What percentage of those classes, do you think, will do much reading before next week's reading period? If the answer isn't 100% then you know a reading period is a serious no-no.

The only way any of us ever becomes a reader is through self-discovery. We may have had books around us at home, or relatives who bought them every birthday and Christmas whether we asked for them or not. We may have had friends who talked about books. We were allowed to quit books if we didn't like them. We were given the space to choose our own, rubbish or not, without an adult sneering at our choice. From there, we persisted and developed the confidence to read more challenging books. That's the way it works. But some kids don't have those experiences, and it is our responsibility as English teachers to provide them. Reading every day is the best way to create that habit. Please don't leave it to chance.

My experiences as a secondary school English teacher convince me that those who don't read for pleasure, not at all coincidentally, are also those who most struggle with examinations in the upper school. They'll often recognise this in retrospect and wish they had time machines to take them back to S1/Year 8 so they could begin to read. But it is worth asking ourselves whether, as English teachers, we (willingly or not) actively discourage kids from reading. Think about it: book reviews, having to read 'classics' that are way beyond their ability or interest levels, reading periods.

A LITTLE PROJECT OR TWO

Getting your class involved in some project-based work can be really effective if there is a genuine purpose to it. For some years now, the Scottish Book Trust have organised author visits which have proven to be immensely successful.[5] Meeting a real live writer can be inspirational for young people. They hear a real writer reading; they can be inspired to write for themselves; they read more as a result.

I've always found that making use of outside contacts can be really helpful. Having worked closely with the initial teacher training department of the University of Strathclyde, I get to speak to trainee teachers every year.[6] Recently, I approached a group of thirty trainee teachers to ask whether they would be willing to be pen pals to a young S1/Year 8 class.

I make a big play about building these guys up as willing pen pals. What's a pen pal? What might be the purpose? Why might we want to write a letter to a stranger? Letter writing feels such an archaic form of communication nowadays, and I struggle to think of the last time I had to write one. But there's something about them that I still love: the secrecy of the envelope, the address, the stamp, the anticipation of a reply, the paper. My god, the paper! And the handwriting.

---

5   See http://www.scottishbooktrust.com/learning/live-literature-programme/
    support-for-events.
6   Hat tip to the amazing Raymond Soltysek, Linda Harris and Hugh Gallagher.

The children write letters about their reading: the books they like, why they like them, the amount of reading they do. The kids love it; I think it's the idea that a real person will read and respond to their feelings – and without a red pen in sight. The trainee teachers love it too because, even though they are really busy, they get to engage with kids about something that, hopefully, they genuinely enjoy. The trembling sense of anticipation when the letters come back is tangible. The kids tear the envelopes open and can't wait to get stuck in to the replies.

And that first reply, the first time that it really sinks in that this is a real person and not a fictional character made up by the teacher, really gets them going. Second letters are better than the first; third letters are even better. That's about as much as we can do over three teaching placements. But if you can keep copies of their letters throughout the year, you'll see a lot of improvement. This is genuine writing about their reading. They feel the responsibility to write loads in the letters; and by the end of the year they've read loads too.

Earlier in this chapter, I stated that kids need to see value in reading if they're to embed it as a habit. This project helps them along the way because it is long term, real and insists that they read and discuss their reading. We're taking our reading out of the classroom. We're using adult readers as our audience.

Now, where else might I find some adults who could talk about their reading?

PUBLISH AND BE DAMNED!

There are over 120 members of teaching staff in my school. With support staff there may well be 150. Many of them even read books! What a great source to have on your doorstep! I have already suggested that encouraging your classes to speak to other teachers about their reading can be highly effective. It's not just the crusty old English teachers who bang on about books! But there is also a very public way to tap into this resource: a great little project which raises the profile of reading for pleasure in your school.

Why not create an e-book about staff reading that is researched, written and developed by your students? Technology has advanced so much that you no longer need to fund an overly expensive paper copy, produced by some fly-by-night shysters who rub their hands with glee at the thought of the school budget. At the click of a few buttons – and let's face it, the kids are generally way ahead of us on this – you can create a school book every year if you like. It takes a bit of thought and planning, but the project more or less takes care of itself, and you can sit back and enjoy watching it unfold.

I send out a whole school e-mail, asking the staff what their favourite book was when they were growing up. The responses come flooding back; it's an opportunity to return to childhood classics for some, a nostalgic sigh for others. You'll be amazed at some of the suggestions which sometimes come from the more unexpected sources: *Little Women*, *The Phantom Tollbooth*, *The Secret Diary of Adrian Mole*. There is no reason to be surprised that educated people would have their own reading histories, but after seventeen years in my school, I have begun to see another side to my colleagues.

At this point, each of your students (I have thirty in my class) can either pick teachers from the list or you can draw names out of a hat. Each student has a teacher to interview, and they will each have a page in the book. Their job is to construct appropriate questions, approach and interview the teacher, then write, edit and submit their page to an editorial team, who may have been chosen by the teacher or elected by the children. They could take a photograph of the teacher reading their chosen book, in a comedic pose if possible, and away we go.

Compiling the book is easy. There are lots of programmes available for this purpose: iBooks Author and Active Textbook are ones I've used.[7] They're free, you can upload pages to them very simply and they are easy to share. No money need ever change hands. The book can be e-mailed to everyone and easily viewed – *and* you're raising the profile of reading for pleasure in the school. Even placing photographs of teachers reading on noticeboards around the school spreads the word that 'this is a reading school'.

LEAVING A TRAIL

Far be it for me to comment on what your school does, but you may be one of those enthusiastic English departments who like to dress up as book characters on World Book Day (other celebratory days are available), and that's fine with me. They look like lots of fun. It's just that, well, I'm not really sure how teachers dressing up as Gandalf encourages kids to read for pleasure. That's absolutely not a criticism (I think). Perhaps I'm merely scarred from my own disappointing experience of going to the expense of purchasing a Rodion Raskolnikov outfit on eBay and having to explain who I was. To everyone. Never again.

What does make a great little project, however, is to get the children to create video trailers for the books they're reading. This isn't as facile or as fun as it might sound at first. It's a challenge to get them right, but if you can inject some genuine literacy work into the project then you can really stretch the kids to produce some clever and creative work. Get them to narrate their own written work with that deep and dramatic voiceover style you hear on the trailers for Hollywood blockbusters.

---

7   See http://www.apple.com/uk/ibooks-author/ and https://activetextbook.com/.

A few years back the Scottish Book Trust produced some excellent materials to help with the creation of book trailers.[8] By breaking the task down into small details, the resources enable the students to analyse some excellent examples and, along with close analysis of current film trailers, they have all they need to create their own. That deconstruction of the form takes some time, though, if you want genuinely creative work; but, again, it's another project which, once the initial set-up has been done, allows you to sit back, watch and enjoy. Small groups discuss the parts of the book they would like to use. Which scenes? Which characters? What is it that we like about film trailers? The tease? The questions they leave us with? Clearly, they're tempting us to go and see the film, just as book trailers should make people want to read the book.

I try to keep groups to a maximum of three but, if you can get everyone to do their own, all the better. More than three and you get those who are along for the ride (like Bez from the Happy Mondays – he's there and having a great time, but nobody knows why). This is a common problem with group-work in general. There will be scripts to write, soundtracks to create and props to find. There are even some nice computer programs which can be used, like iMovie, iMotion or Magisto. They can film it on a smartphone and edit it on said phone. No problem.

The pay-off comes when you organise the big premiere! Get some popcorn in and make a big deal of their work. Ask each group to present their submissions, explaining which books they've chosen and why. Their trailers can be kept to use as future inspiration and recommendations for subsequent classes.

You can cover so many bases with book trailers: reading, writing, talking and listening. However, as always, reading is right at the heart of the task.

---

8   See http://www.scottishbooktrust.com/video-tags/book-trailer-masterclass.

UNBREAKING THE HABIT OF A LIFETIME

I started this chapter by referencing Charles Duhigg's cue, routine, reward analysis of our habits and, hopefully, I've suggested some ways in which we can use this as a way of getting kids to read. The routine part must always be reading, and the cue needs to be the same every time. That special time to read – for me, the beginning of a lesson – needs to be recognisable, expected and as regular as possible. The children need someone to inform them about the best books for them: someone who knows them well enough to match them up with the perfect book, especially the boys. And that someone, my friend, is you.

Chapter 9
BOYS 'N' BOOKS

The e-book project described in the previous chapter revealed some traditional children's choices among the staff favourites: *Anne of Green Gables*, *Alice's Adventures in Wonderland*, the 'Famous Five' books. You get the picture. Alongside the top picks of my current set of 12-year-olds – *The Hunger Games*, *The Maze Runner*, *The Boy in the Striped Pyjamas* – I began to notice a particular theme. The more popular books with young readers appear to be those in which there are no adults around, certainly when the main action occurs. And when they do appear, they tend to be evil and very much to be avoided. Fair advice. We tend to forget this when we, ourselves, become adults.

The bizarrely simple middle-class lives of the Famous Five or the Secret Seven crowd were so far away from my mundane, unadventurous, cold summers in the west of Scotland in the seventies, yet I hoovered them up as if I was scared that I'd lose them forever. The adult-free world of secret meetings in the garden shed and specially created written codes were fabulous to behold, even if it took days to decipher my mate's, 'Can I borrow your *Beano* annual?' Of course, I'd avoid the complications of a reply and just hand it to him. He'd earned it.

Sad to say, in my experience anyway, Enid Blyton doesn't fly so well with today's kids. Not when they can run around killing people with Katniss Everdeen in *The Hunger Games*. Her mostly adult-free world is one of survival; it is a world which many kids recognise. She must use her skills – skills hitherto unknown to her family and unexpected by those adults who want to get rid of her – to overcome a series of problems that she has been plunged into by the fascistic, authoritarian society of grown-ups. Julian, Dick, Anne, George and Timmy wouldn't have lasted five minutes in such a place. The Secret Seven even less.

What's clear though – and it is something that's difficult to ignore when recommending books to children – is that it has always been the same: kids like reading books about kids. They like those kids to be close to their age, not necessarily from similar backgrounds, but to experience the horror of school, the worries about fitting in, the problems of growing up. They want characters who have friends they can turn to, adults to hate (especially teachers!) and happy endings ... eventually. Yes, they want to enter strange worlds, but they also want to hang out with their friends for as long as possible. So they love the relationship between Bruno and Shmuel; they prefer to see Michael with Mina in *Skellig* but kind of like it when his mates come round; Frodo can't get where he needs to go without his friends.

This world of friendship forms the heart of much of children's literature, where kids are left alone to get on with things. The recent explosion in the world of teen fiction continues with that theme more vigorously than ever – from the books of Jacqueline Wilson to Charlie Higson's 'Young Bond' series and the new 'Sherlock Holmes' series. But it would be remiss of me not to discuss the greatest literary sensation of our generation: Mr Potter, please take a step forward.

THE POTTER FACTOR

You don't need me to tell you about J. K. Rowling and her phenomenal success. You'd be hard pressed to find someone who hasn't heard of her chief character. Are the books brilliantly written? Possibly not. Would they stand up to the quality of classic children's literature of the past? Maybe not. Do they nail absolutely everything that makes kids' books great? Absolutely – in spades.

The 'Harry Potter' books captured their audience because – and I've no doubt J. K. Rowling was aware of this – they tick every one of the boxes I mentioned earlier. Kids away from adults? Check. Seemingly insurmountable challenges to overcome? Check. Friendship required to overcome said problems? Check. Set in a school? Check. The reasonably simple good versus evil narrative reflects a desire to see our friends triumph over adversity, at least most of the time. Following Harry's friends through every year of school as they experience love and hate, life and death – and at the same time seeing their faces on every available space in our high streets, especially after the movies started coming out (I struggle to recall anything which has had more product placement) – was the perfect mix of great children's literature.

While the last few years has seen a real drop-off in the number of kids bringing 'Harry Potter' books into class, the pleasing thing is that they've been replaced by a steady flow of teen fiction following in J. K. Rowling's immense shadow. Of course, there have been book series around for ages, but the 'Harry Potter' books appear to have given birth to a tsunami of three, four, five and six book cash cows: 'The Hunger Games' trilogy, Michael Grant's 'Gone' series and the astonishing 'Chaos Walking' series from Patrick Ness. All challenging and engaging in equal measure: clever writing which respects the intelligence of teens looking for a bridge between child and adult reading. None of them would have been anywhere near as successful as they are without the Potter child.

While we have our reluctant readers in mind, then, what can we take from this trend that can influence our choice of class library? Forget the books you read as a child, to begin with anyway. It might be difficult for you to swallow but C. S. Lewis won't entice reluctant readers today – the language is too complex. The same with *The Wind in the Willows*. It's a wonderful book but your 'reading haters' won't get past Mole's first sniffles. What, most of all, attracts readers to the 'Harry Potter' series? The movies. Well, there are other movies. Don't turn your nose up at a book which has been made into a film. Even if they've seen the film, their knowledge of the story may help them along in their reading.

Judge a book by its cover. Why not? We like things which appeal to the eye. Books can be beautiful and aesthetically pleasing. However, more importantly, if you are to be the one who recommends books – the person children turn to when they need a book suggestion – then you need to have read some of them yourself.

WHICH AUTHORS?

There's a real problem if you take your class to the library and all you can suggest to them are the books you read when you were their age. Not to say they aren't great books, of course they are. But therein lies the rub. They're yours. And you're old! And the books are old! Whether we like it or not, we need a good grasp of what's doing the rounds now if our reluctant readers are to take you seriously. Good quality, up-to-date teen fiction is a total must for your class library. Pick them up whenever you can; have them on your desk; offer them up to the best readers first; create a buzz. But, most importantly, read them yourself. Here's just a short list of the most read writers in my classes.

Marcus Sedgwick

Marcus Sedgwick's books are beautifully haunting, often historical; they create mysterious worlds which don't patronise readers. *White Crow* tends to

114

capture the interest of girls with its surreal interleaving of past and present. *Revolver* is a thrillingly exciting tale set in the Arctic Circle a hundred years ago: a young boy is stuck in a cabin in the middle of nowhere when he hears a knock on the door. Along with *Midwinterblood, My Swordhand is Singing* and a bunch of others, Marcus Sedgwick is one of the best writers around.

Sophie McKenzie

There's a struggle to get enough books by Sophie McKenzie into our school library. Again, the girls love them and hoover them up whenever they find them on the shelves. McKenzie is a prolific writer of thrillers which grab you by the throat and hold on until the end. Her 'Missing' series is extraordinary, but 'The Medusa Project' and 'Blood Ties' series are also guaranteed winners in the classroom. She captures a sense of realism that teens recognise, and characters who could be living their lives. And did I mention prolific – very prolific.

Patrick Ness

I've not been struck by any series more than Ness' 'Chaos Walking' trilogy. They are books that create a new language and a new world to which we can immediately relate, with characters who are faced with a desperate search for survival. These are all familiar themes, with young characters set against evil adults in power. They are long books, however, which often concerns me with teen fiction, so they're not for everyone. Even Harry Potter's final adventures were unnecessarily long for kids. Ness' books are glorious though. Have them in your classroom.

Mal Peet

It took me an awfully long time to find teen fiction about football that was any good. At school, I read Michael Hardcastle novels: tales of unexpected cup runs or hero worshipping, last minute penalty kick winners. Having searched them out recently I found they were awful! Mal Peet's 'Paul Faustino' series is a wonderful thing though. Intelligent football fiction, peppered with intrigue, they fill a huge gap for smart boys who might be looking for challenging reading.

You also have Dan Freedman who writes much simpler, yet still enjoyable, books about football. And boys read them again and again.

You should also check out Catherine MacPhail, David Almond, Kevin Brooks, Theresa Breslin, Celia Rees and Meg Rosoff – all great writers who have mastered teen fiction. And that's no easy feat, especially when it comes to engaging boys in reading.

BOYS DON'T READ?

Boys, eh? What can you do? What's the point in trying to get them to read? It's just too much trouble.

It's so easy to accept lazy, stupid clichés and give up on the little monsters just at the time when they need us most. Our failure to develop a love of reading in boys contributes to literacy issues which will live with them forever. But I have no doubt that they will read if we stick with them; if we remain patient with their often aggressive resistance to reading of any kind and never forget the importance of reading for their future employment. Indeed, our inability to convince some boys of the importance of literacy in their lives perhaps stems from our lack of awareness of their interests outside of school. As Mihaly Csikszentmihalyi asks, if literacy is for the sake of the children, how come we so rarely bother to find out what they want to use it for?[1]

When we understand what literacy is for, we can start to appreciate why boys make instantaneous judgements about the reading we give them. When we begin to connect with their own interests and 'front load' the reading we ask them to do, then we can begin to anticipate the subjects they will accept and appreciate. And that takes more than merely referring to their interest inventories (see Chapter 2). It means that we must know them and keep talking to them about books. It means finding articles and websites and information which will open them up to new thoughts and experiences. It means finding fiction that will grab them, and finding more of the same when it does. But whatever you do, don't give up on them; don't dismiss them for not reading or punish them with the dreaded 'non-reader' label.

Why is it that boys can lose themselves in the narrative of computer games but not in that of a book? Perhaps because there are difficulties to overcome in a game, and there are fairly clear consequences for each decision they make. But we make mistakes when we try to take that recipe and transfer it wholesale to books. We patronise boys and undervalue them when we fall into the trap of providing only non-fiction texts for them, when we lazily decide to give them reading material that only relates to their interests.

Of course, this is a way in. But it's only a very small step on the long path to creating a reader. Boys – and this chapter is all about boys – often have such varied interests that we can stereotypically side-line many of the things they value, and our inept attempts to engage them can turn them off reading even more. We convince ourselves that by taking them to the library or

---

1   M. Csikszentmihalyi, Literacy and intrinsic motivation, *Daedalus* 119(2) (spring 1990): 115–140.

offering them free access to books on our classroom shelves we are offering them a choice about what they might read. But we fail to realise that choice is not *real* choice when it's limited to what books the school has to offer; too often they don't value what the school has to offer. And when they don't have much of a choice outside of school either, that leaves us in a bit of a predicament.

BEING THE MODEL READER

One of the most important things I hope you will take away from reading this book is an awareness that you are a role model for the youngsters in your care, especially when it comes to promoting reading for pleasure. I never underestimate this role. Some of the kids I teach don't go home to shelves of books. Or even to shelves. I may well be the only significant reader in their lives; for example, many may never have seen an older male read at home. If you find yourself in that position, then you really need to take this responsibility seriously. How can I offer these guys a real choice? How can I convince them that reading is something I do for pleasure and not something I want to impose upon them?

> If we want our students to read and enjoy it for the rest of their lives then we must show them what a reading life looks like.
>
> Donalyn Miller[2]

Boys like having the ability to choose what they read, but this needs to be tempered with the teacher's knowledge of what may be good and worthwhile to read. Creating the conditions for boys to feel that they have control over what they read can come when you read great books in front of them;

---

2   Miller, *The Book Whisperer*, p. 110.

118

when you enthuse about the subjects they enjoy, characters they may like and situations which may be familiar. More importantly, you should be very confident that the books you offer them will be accessible and rewarding. Steven Layne warns that 'a larger and larger percentage of students haven't had enough positive experiences with literature in school to foster a desire to spend any time with books'.[3] Early experiences of reading need to be positive ones for boys. And, more importantly, shared.

In his wonderful book, *Breaking Through Barriers to Boys' Achievement*, Gary Wilson claims that we 'continue to force boys to read and write before they are mentally and physically capable'.[4] By the time they get to me at the age of 11, I would be concerned if they weren't physically ready to read, but I get the mentally ready part. Where we come in is to prepare that state of mental readiness.

In Chapter 3 I discussed using magazine subscriptions as a way for parents to engage their children in reading. Whatever the topic, surrounding them with accessible reading material is always a good thing. However, as they read more and more, I'd be wary of an over-emphasis on non-fiction. Their obsession with *Guinness World Records* or skateboarding magazines is fine in principle, but it ignores the importance of fiction and why we read it.

Gary Wilson argues that 'boys need to read fiction because boys desperately need all the help they can get to help them REFLECT'.[5] Reading about fictional characters allows them to develop empathy, something in which boys can be lacking. Even getting them to reflect on those characters' situations can help them to address their thoughts and feelings about their own lives. And isn't that, ultimately, why we all read – to widen our experiences of life? To place ourselves in the shoes of characters who have to deal with

3   Layne, *Igniting a Passion for Reading*, p. 13.
4   Wilson, *Breaking Through Barriers to Boys' Achievement*, p. 7.
5   Wilson, *Breaking Through Barriers to Boys' Achievement*, p. 32.

complications in their lives? Accepting that boys don't read fiction is unfair in so many ways. Get them excited about the books you suggest to them and they'll wolf 'em down.

Wilson writes about a school library he knew where they kept new books behind barbed wire, with warning signs and 'Danger!' all over them. 'When a few weeks later it was announced that they would now be available for loan at such and such a time, there was a queue from the dining room to the library.'[6] You can begin to see the possibilities. Allow boys to choose – and buy – books for the library. Get them to create their own newsletter for boys' books only. Give them jobs in the library, issuing books or organising shelves – make it their space too.

SMALL STEPS FOR BOYS, GIANT STEPS FOR BOYKIND

Transforming boys into readers is a remarkable thing, and it will change their lives. It can be done, too, if you really believe it's worthwhile, possible and important. Consider this: according to PISA, 'in OECD countries, boys are on average 39 points behind girls in reading, the equivalent of one year of schooling'.[7] The fact that we're not moving heaven and earth to narrow that gap is more staggering than the figure itself. Spend some time tomorrow thinking about each boy in your class and what you can do to start their reading journey.

Some of the strategies in this book should help you on your way. I've suggested that ten minutes of reading a day is a great way to start any lesson.

---

6   Wilson, *Breaking Through Barriers to Boys' Achievement*, p. 35.

7   Department for Education, Research Evidence On Reading for Pleasure, p. 18.

Consistent approaches to providing daily time, in short doses, gets everyone reading. Boys enjoy the regularity and many even enjoy the silence, albeit only for a short time. But these brief bursts of reading add up, and turn into books that have been read, lists that have been made and small steps to achievement which you can build on. Making a big deal of the lad who finishes a book on his own, perhaps for the first time, might make him outwardly cringe, but inside he's glowing with pride.

What you will begin to see are boys who take ownership of their reading. Reading another book on top of the first one adds to the building blocks of a reading history. This reading thing loses its 'otherness' and becomes something they too can be a part of. If you break down the barriers of difficulty for boys then they start to see themselves as readers, because 'Students who believe they can read well are going to read often.'[8] The importance of getting them in the 'game' is huge. Moving beyond the often simplistic world of short non-fiction texts, or even graphic novels, which do 'not correlate positively with higher levels of literacy',[9] shows that you genuinely care about their literacy.

Hopefully, you're on your way to creating a class full of readers. Readers who take responsibility for their choices, who go home and read and are happy to share that reading with others. As their English teacher, I may well never see the fruits of my labour – I want them to be readers in ten, twenty, thirty years' time. But in the short term we can make the experience of reading

---

8   A. McRae and J. T. Guthrie, Promoting reasons for reading: teacher practices that impact motivation, in E. H. Hiebert (ed.), *Reading More, Reading Better* (New York: Guilford Press, 2009), pp. 55–76 at p. 63.
9   L. Allen, J. Cipielewski and K. E. Stanovich, Multiple indicators of children's reading habits and attitudes: construct validity and cognitive correlates, *Journal of Educational Psychology* 84(a4): 489–503, cited in B. E. Cullinan, Independent reading and school achievement, *Research Journal of the American Association of School Librarians* 3 (2000). Available at: http://www.ala.org/aasl/sites/ala.org.aasl/files/content/aaslpubsandjournals/slr/vol3/SLMR_IndependentReading_V3.pdf.

as pleasurable as possible and, of course, make it a central part of our curriculum. To do that, though, we must be able to link it to everyday classwork. Remember that?

Chapter 10
EVERY DAY'S A READING DAY

Polonius: What do you read, my lord?

Hamlet: Words, words, words.

Hamlet, II. ii

Please don't be mistaken and imagine my working day is spent knee-high in books, quoting liberally from Dickens at uncomprehending students and obsessing about reading for pleasure. If only it were so. In truth, I am little more than a bedraggled, wilting, full-time teacher of English who turns up every day to deal with the same time constraints and the same meaningless paperwork as anyone else. I have classes to prepare for end-of-year exams; I have five sets of kids marching merrily along the corridor to see me most days – that's 150 kids a day. They write and write and moan and complain and read and read and moan and complain and do more writing. And I mark that writing. Boy, do I mark that writing! My focus on reading for pleasure has to be incorporated into the curriculum I am told I must follow.

I make time for it. It's not the sole focus of my day.

But if it were, my day might look something like this …

I'd arrive early for school, around 8 o'clock. I like that hour or so of quiet before the hurricane of kids turns up. It's Monday, so I have a few new books I've picked up over the weekend. A shiny copy of *Wonder* by R. J. Palacio and second-hand copies of Anthony Horowitz's 'The Diamond Brothers' series. I place them, standing proud, at the front of my desk and wait for the first desperate hands to grab them. With my first coffee of the day, I put my feet up and browse through a few of the kids' reading dialogue journals. I try to keep on top of these, but it's impossible to read them all every week, so working through a small pile every so often allows me to see who's into what and who's ready to move on to something more challenging. I might write a short note in reply if there is any confusion, or if I'd like Tom to give me a bit more. No matter how long I've been doing this, it's always a lovely feeling when kids write to you about their books. And even the ones who are too cool to write 'Dear Mr P' still like to know I've read their thoughts. I spend about twenty minutes (perhaps half an hour) on these every so often to assuage the guilt of not marking enough books last night.

But S2/Year 9 are due in just after 9 o'clock. It's their weekly library visit, so they'll take their journals with them. A couple couldn't quite finish their entries last week – chatting about the football perhaps? – so I put them aside to remind them. They will have read further on in their books by now, so I try to have a little informal chat with them on our way upstairs. Claire struggles to recall what happened in her book this week – she wasn't really reading, just glossing – so I politely suggest she takes a few moments to read back over this week's chapters. When we get to the library, I prefer them to spend as much time reading or finding a new book as possible, as we only get one visit a week. I have to guide a couple of the boys in a more productive direction and make a few suggestions. They take three, sometimes four, books to their seats and read the opening pages of all of them. They then pick one or two to take back downstairs with them. On the way, we chat about this week's choices, and I make sure I speak to everyone if possible.

I'm well prepared for the unruly S3/Year 10 who arrive reluctantly and sporadically from PE. They are as truculent as you might imagine to begin with but soon calm down. I've placed their books on their desks and we settle in to ten minutes of reading. It's a habit I won't drop despite their early reluctance, and it's beginning to pay off. Most read; one or two refuse; another pretends. But they no longer interrupt others, so I'm getting there bit by bit, one by one. The buzzer goes at the end of ten minutes and they all close their books. They have been working on 100 word book reviews and I have an example on the whiteboard. No book title or author; no 'A book I have read ...' They start with the character's name and move on. No spoilers but accurate spelling and punctuation. They find it challenging when I send them back huffily to their desks with corrections, but their work, eventually, will look great on the corridor wall directly outside the classroom.

It's morning interval next: I have to wheel the movable store of computers for S1/Year 8 along the corridor. The laptops can be unreliable and the Wi-Fi is often patchy, so I place them on the desks and check the connectivity of each one as I go. The more prepared we are, the more we can get through. I ask them to log in and then do their ten minutes of reading, so the whirring ancient technology is set up in time for the rest of the lesson. Yes, I know, it's 2016! They have been adding entries to our 'Bookworm Blog' and need to find thumbnails of the books to place on their posts; some have recorded their short reviews so they can add them as a podcast. I spend most of the period holding my breath, hoping the Wi-Fi holds up along with the battery life, and we can get everyone's work up on the blog. But the lesson takes care of itself without much input from me at this point. We manage to finish up, log off and return the laptops to the store before the bell goes. They leave happy.

I have some non-contact time now and, as well as topping up with coffee having missed my break, I try to catch up with another couple of kids' journals. I notice that James has finished all of the Mal Peet books apart from one, so I try to hunt down a second-hand copy on Amazon or eBay. As a rule, I'm not too crazy about teachers spending their own money on school supplies. In a time of massive cutbacks this could be a very dangerous road down which to travel; what starts as a nice thing to do rapidly turns into a necessary expense. However, I often make an exception for books. James started the year proud of being a non-reader. This year has changed him, so ensuring that he has no periods without a book he likes is my attempt to keep the momentum up. This particular book is also one I've not read, so I can talk to him about it and push him along with it.

After lunch I see S5/Year 12: we're reading a Nabokov short story in preparation for exams and looking at ways to understand new vocabulary through context. They don't seem to be grasping the concept or developing any proper strategies. I reach for my own book. I've been reading *Austerlitz* by W. G. Sebald and came across this passage last night: 'The construction of fortifications ... clearly showed how we feel obliged to keep surrounding ourselves with defences, built in successive phases as a precaution against any incursion by enemy powers ...'[1]

I write it on the board and they struggle with 'fortifications' and 'incursion'. Once we get into 'enemy powers' and 'surrounding ourselves' they begin to get the idea of fortifications. Once they've done that it doesn't take long for them to arrive at a meaning of 'incursion'. The whole 'mini-lesson' takes about ten minutes; I ask them now to take out their own books and find examples of words and passages they don't understand. They begin to see the real purpose of developing their reading skills both in reading for pleasure and in exam preparation.

The last class of the day is with S4/Year 11. They have a big assessment coming up and are anxious to get to work on revision. We get there but, even at our most frantic moments, I insist that they read for ten minutes at the beginning of the lesson. The silence calms them, gets them into the thinking zone and allows them to focus on learning. We put our books away and get on with the lesson.

---

1   W. G. Sebald, *Austerlitz* (London: Penguin, 2001), p. 100.

'LITERACY ... IS A BULWARK AGAINST POVERTY [AND] A PLATFORM FOR DEMOCRATIZATION'[2]

So, we're almost finished. The part of the book in your right hand is significantly shorter than the part in your left. Unless you're reading it on an e-reader, in which case you might be at about 90%. Who really knows what's coming? Hopefully, you'll already have one eye on the next book on your list. Perhaps reading this little cracker will have encouraged you to look again at your approach to reading for pleasure in your classroom. I do hope so. But please remember that, while it's impossible to force anyone to enjoy reading, for pleasure or for any other reason, and while that perhaps is not the sole purpose of your job as a teacher, the children in your care will be affected, perhaps for ever more, by their access or lack of access to books.

So it's not too much of a stretch to say that getting children to read and enjoy reading is one of the most important things that we should be doing at school. French writer Daniel Pennac's *The Rights of the Reader* provides a good starting point for a final discussion. The rights are:

1 The right not to read.

2 The right to skip.

3 The right not to finish a book.

4 The right to read it again.

5 The right to read anything.

---

2   United Nations, Secretary-general stresses need for political will and resources to meet challenge of fight against illiteracy (press release, 8 September 1997). Available at: http://www.un.org/press/en/1997/19970904.SGSM6316.html.

6   The right to mistake a book for real life.

7   The right to read anywhere.

8   The right to dip in.

9   The right to read out loud.

10   The right to be quiet.

So here's what I think:

1. The right not to read

Okay, I have a problem with the first one. Bad start, I know. By all means, if you're at home, then put your book down. In my class, I give you ten minutes and I expect you to use it constructively. If you don't have a book, I'll get you one. If you're bored with your book, I'll allow you to change it (see right number 3). But you will read during those ten minutes. Oh yes, you will read. I only have fifty minutes a day with you and much of that is taken up with the rest of the hugely packed curriculum. So let's not waste it.

2. The right to skip

Again, a tricky one. My lifetime confession is that, for years, I lied about reading all of *Moby Dick*. It has been said that six months after reading one of the classics you can barely remember more than what was in the blurb. I used that excuse with the big whale book. Much of it was deathly dull. Bones 'n' all that. I skipped like a gleeful schoolgirl. So, I'd be a hypocrite to deny some skipping in the classroom. Just don't make a habit of it. I want you to know the difference between a good book and a bad book and for you to be able to explain it. So, move along quickly.

3. The right not to finish a book

I've got an excuse for this. I'm turning 50 and don't have the time to waste any more. I now judge the readability of a book not by reviews, but by its width. More than 300 pages? Maybe not. I've no issue with dumping books, but in class I ensure that at least thirty pages have been read. Have they given it time? Have they tried? What can they tell me about the opening? Life is too short to squander on bad books, but give them a chance, eh!

4. The right to read it again

We return to our favourites for comfort like revisiting an old friend. I know Holden Caulfield will be there for me, still lost, sitting on a bench, watching Phoebe on the carousel. Rereading a book is often a necessity as we 'strive to calculate how best to maintain the magic'.[3] So Gemma can read *Harry Potter and the Philosopher's Stone* for the seventh time and Sean can laugh out loud again at *Skulduggery Pleasant*. It's their chill zone, their hook to hang their coat on. But keep checking in and moving them on.

---

3   Jacobs, *The Pleasures of Reading In An Age of Distraction* p. 34.

5. The right to read anything

There is always one kid who attempts to take something inappropriate from the library. It's not merely that the subject matter may be a little suspect – I do think we need to have some editorial control over what they choose – but the level of difficulty also needs to be right. Fine, read a book that is too hard for you, but don't pick the popular 'fantasy' series which is 700 pages long and weighs more than the rest of your schoolbag, particularly when your last book was *Diary of a Wimpy Kid*. Read a few pages before you commit, then decide.

6. The right to mistake a book for real life

Pennac calls the right to mistake a book for real life a 'textually transmitted disease'.[4] I once spent several days carrying a dice in my pocket after reading Luke Rhinehart's *The Dice Man*. Explaining it away to friends was tricky, but it seemed like the rational thing to do at the time. Roll a dice to decide every decision in your day. What could possibly go wrong? Identifying with the main character in the novel you're reading is a perfectly natural thing to do, especially if you're 12. These guys are your pals, your confidants. I soon put my dice away and moved on to something else. But it was great for a day or two.

---

4   Pennac, *The Rights of the Reader*, p. 163.

7. The right to read anywhere

I always try to have extension work for kids who rattle through the less challenging parts of the lessons I create, but if I don't have such work readily available, I'm happy for them to pick up their books and get a few more pages in. 'Any chance I can' is a message I want them to remember wherever they are. One of the great advantages of having a Kindle is that if I'm out and about, and I can't fit my book in my pocket, then I've always got something to read. I've read up mountains and at sea, on planes and waiting in cars. Encourage kids to have a book with them at all times. After a while it will become second nature.

8. The right to dip in

Part of the pleasure of having a reasonably large book collection is the aesthetic joy I feel as I sit in front of them in semi-worship. I run my hands along their spines, pulling out books that I read long ago, entering their lost worlds and revisiting places I once knew well. In the library, I ask kids to pick up three, four or five books and read the first page or two of all of them. They may get a taste of three great books or two terrible ones. However, they're dipping in and out, and that's what readers do: 'When you don't have the time or the means to treat yourself to a week in Venice, why not spend five minutes there.'[5]

---

5   Pennac, *The Rights of the Reader*, p. 168.

9. The right to read out loud

I had a story published by the Scottish Book Trust recently and was invited to read it at the launch of the collection.[6] Even though I've been teaching a long while, and read out loud most days, I hardly slept for a week. By the time I arrived at the venue I was sick with nerves and wanted to pull out. It was magnificent though. When you read out loud the words come alive in a way you could never predict. It's why asking kids to read essays out loud or record themselves is such an effective way of noticing errors. Encouraging them to read aloud from their books is not only an essential way of checking for fluency and understanding, but it also raises stories to another level. Go immediately and get your book and read a page out loud. You'll see, or hear.

10. The right to be quiet

Okay. We're almost at the very end. I'll be quiet now; I'm off to read my book. But there's a final truism I must broach: that a quiet classroom is in some ways an old-fashioned one. However, the only way anyone develops a real love of reading is by sitting quietly with a book. The myth that kids tend not to see reading as something they would choose over, say, playing on their games consoles does have some truth in it. But how often do we allow them to sit in silence in classes these days? With our desks in groups and our cooperative learning strategies in place, it seems that to look into a classroom and see thirty 11-year-olds sitting reading in silence ain't 'sexy' teaching.

The reality is that it's more than likely that half of the class engaged in noisy groupwork are secretly wishing that they could be sitting in silence, given

---

6   Oh, go on, read it. Humour me: http://www.scottishbooktrust.com/reading/stories-of-home/story/the-good-shepherd.

the peace to get on with things, unencumbered by the nonsense of the day, the distractions of the class clowns and the teacher droning on. In secondary school, any protected time during which the students read in silence can be a real joy. It can provide the only opportunity for me to chat quietly to those who need it most and to intervene on a one-to-one basis. It's lovely and calm and, although they are sometimes grudging about that appreciation, it does exist.

It's why our libraries should be libraries and not information centres or cafes. It's why our classrooms need not always be noisy and collaborative. We think best when we are silent. We might learn best when we are silent. So, for at least some time during our day, let's be silent.

> This morning, I looked at the books on my shelves and thought that they have no knowledge of my existence. They come to life because I open them and turn their pages, and yet they don't know that I am their reader.
>
> Alberto Manguel[7]

READING ALOUD ALLOWED

One of the most fulfilling things I do as an English teacher, one of the things I look forward to most, is reading great writing aloud. Not always great novels, but I have to admit it is this which pleases me most. If you've never read to a large group of kids – and I'm clearly not including English teachers in this – then it is a profound experience. The intimacy of the moment, the electricity of the dramatic scene is unique in my job. When you can recreate

---

7   A. Manguel, *A Reading Diary: A Year of Favourite Books*, (Edinburgh: Cannongate, 2006) p. 213.

the tension of a great piece of writing – through hushed tones, genuine anger and subtle nuance – then you hold a class in the palm of your hand.

There are scenes in some of the books I teach which still cause a tingle down my spine. Holden Caulfield's explanation of his desire to be 'the catcher in the rye'; Macduff's reaction on hearing the news of the murder of his family in *Macbeth*; the gripping finale to *Of Mice and Men*; the final, beautiful, poetic last section of *The Great Gatsby*. Every one of them leaves me gulping back a tear, and I've yet to read any of them to a class who haven't been wrapped up in every word. The room is silent. The words sink in. The bell signals the end of the period. They gasp in disappointment. I let them go.

Steven Layne says, 'Every story read to students from any genre contributes to building their background knowledge in some way.'[8] And that knowledge is very often better left alone when the book is finished, for a time anyway. Deliberately *not* stopping reading the book to ask what we thought of it, why did that happen or what does it really mean is an effective way to allow children to think their own thoughts. Leave it alone for a while. No worksheets, no comprehension quizzes, no wasting time on activities that show we have done something when all we have done is ruin the experience. Let it settle. Then talk.

If we are to create lifelong readers then it is important that we don't cast them adrift with meaningless, time-consuming nonsense. Yes, we look at great writing and analyse and discuss it. But we need to ask ourselves what we want most of all at the end of the process: readers who *can* access difficult texts, or readers who *do* access difficult texts? Unless we promote reading as something to be enjoyed in and out of school, something which they will take with them for the rest of their lives, then we are in danger of creating a generation of Donalyn Miller's 'aliterate' children: we can read, but reading wasn't enjoyable at school, so we choose not to.

8   Layne, *Igniting a Passion for Reading*, p. 61.

When I read out loud to kids I am reminded why I wanted to teach in the first place. I have memories of my English teacher reading the chapter from *Lord of the Flies* in which Piggy meets his doom; I went out and bought the book that weekend! I may still have the same copy all these years later. Even so, I can still hear the teacher's voice slightly cracking as he read the words, probably for the umpteenth time, to a class of previously rowdy teenagers. That stuff never goes away.

In class, we've just finished reading *The Outsiders* by S. E. Hinton. The kids in this group have read more with me than they've ever read. I gave them the time to do it and I talked about books with them. I made sure I found the reluctant ones and let them sit until, together, we found books which engaged them. That is my job as an English teacher.

> The job of adults who care about reading is to move heaven and earth to put that book into a child's hands.
>
> Nancie Atwell[9]

The scene from *The Outsiders* which gets to these kids is not the scene when Johnny dies but when Dally does. Dally, the hard, cold thug; the rebel; the one who cares about nothing, not even himself. His death is so unexpected but so inevitable, there are gasps in the room and cries of 'no'. They gasp because they see themselves in Dally. They empathise with this character. They have learned to do this, and now go off and read their own books. They are learning through reading in class because we have given them the time and space to fall into books. We owe them that.

---

9   Atwell, *The Reading Zone*, p. 28.

LAST WORD

Over the years, as I read more and more about reading, the history of reading and the development of how we read, it has become very clear to me that learning to read is a complex business. As a secondary school teacher, that I get thirty new kids at age 11 who can read – to varying degrees, yes, but very rarely any single kid who cannot read at all – is a minor miracle. The complexities of symbol recognition, joining with other symbols to make words, sentences, paragraphs, stories is the result of so many changes in how our brains function that I bow down to the work of my primary colleagues. Hat tip. You do an incredible job.

The difficulties we experience at secondary level are not, or should not be, concerned with teaching kids to read, but with teaching them to read deeply and creating readers who will do so for pleasure for the rest of their lives. When they struggle to do this, it is often because they have no real bank of knowledge behind them, no real reading histories to hang new things on to. Part of my job, and a fundamental reason why I do it, is to help them get there – just as I did many years ago.

The difference between instruction, which we should leave to the experts (our primary colleagues), and building readers who read for pleasure, is that it can be a long old slog to embed the practices and knowledge required to develop those habits. We struggle and search and sometimes battle to find the right book for the right child. Hopefully, that's what this book has been about. However, it must be about more than that.

Literacy is a political as well as a social act. Learning to read and write competently is a foundation of what it takes to lead a full and active life and to take our place in society. Historically treated as a 'moral virtue', literacy is today 'treated more as a cognitive skill',[1] so creating the environment for children to become readers who read because they enjoy it and value it, must be the backbone of any education. Hopefully, this little book has provided some ideas for how to go about beginning this process.

Finally, if you are in a position where providing reading opportunities is possible, never, ever, let that precious time slip away. There's nothing more important that can't wait. Let them read.

---

1   F. Furedi, *Power of Reading: From Socrates to Twitter* (London: Bloomsbury, 2015), p. 151.

BIBLIOGRAPHY

Allen, L., Cipielewski, J. and Stanovich, K. E. Multiple indicators of children's reading habits and attitudes: construct validity and cognitive correlates, *Journal of Educational Psychology* 84 (a4): 489–503.

Anstice, I. Party manifestos: Tories mention libraries in 2 or 3 sentences, Labour and Greens not at all, *Public Libraries News* (14 April 2015). Available at: http://www. publiclibrariesnews.com/2015/04/party-manifestos-tories-mention-libraries-in-2-or-3-sentences-labour-and-greens-not-at-all.html.

Atwell, N. *In the Middle: New Understandings About Writing, Reading, and Learning*, 2nd edn (Portsmouth, NH: Heinemann, 1998).

Atwell, N. *The Reading Zone: How to Help Kids Become Skilled, Passionate, Habitual, Critical Readers* (New York: Scholastic, 2007).

Brand, S. *How Buildings Learn: What Happens After They're Built* (London: Penguin, 2010).

Buckner, A. *Notebook Connections: Strategies for the Reader's Notebook* (Maine, NY: Stenhouse Publishers, 2009).

Bullhorn. Why libraries are effective instruments for social change, *Urban Librarians Unite* (8 June 2015). Available at: http://urbanlibrariansunite.org/2015/06/08/why-libraries-are-effective-instruments-for-social-change/.

Burn-Murdoch, J. and Wisniewska, A. Scottish referendum: who voted which way and why? *FT Data* (19 September 2014). Available at: http://blogs.ft.com/ftdata/2014/09/19/scottish-referendum-who-voted-which-way/.

Canfield, J. and Hendricks, G. *You've Got to Read This Book!* (New York: Harper Collins, 2007).

Carr, N. *The Shallows: How the Internet Is Changing the Way We Think, Read and Remember* (London: Atlantic Books, 2011).

Clark, C. and Rumbold, K. *Reading for Pleasure: A Research Overview* (London: National Literacy Trust, 2006).

Conservative Party. *The Conservative Party Manifesto 2015: Strong Leadership. A Clear Economic Plan. A Brighter, More Secure Future.* Available at: https://www.conservatives.com/manifesto.

Cowley, S. *The Seven E's of Reading for Pleasure* (Bristol: Sue Cowley Books, 2014).

Csikszentmihalyi, M. Literacy and intrinsic motivation, *Daedalus* 119(2) (spring 1990): 115–140.

Cullinan, B. E. Independent reading and school achievement, *Research Journal of the American Association of School Librarians* 3 (2000). Available at: http://www.ala.org/aasl/sites/ala.org.aasl/files/content/aaslpubsandjournals/slr/vol3/SLMR_IndependentReading_V3.pdf.

Department for Education. Research Evidence On Reading for Pleasure (May 2012). Available at: https://www.gov.uk/government/uploads/system/uploads/attachment_data/file/284286/reading_for_pleasure.pdf.

Didau, D. A heck of a lot of posters, *The Learning Spy* (20 September 2015). Available at: http://www.learningspy.co.uk/featured/posters/.

Dredge, S. Are tablet computers harming our children's ability to read?' *The Guardian* (24 August 2015). Available at: https://www.theguardian.com/technology/2015/aug/24/tablets-apps-harm-help-children-read.

Duhigg, C. *The Power of Habit: Why We Do What We Do and How to Change* (London: Heinemann, 2012).

Edmundson, M. *Teacher: The One Who Made the Difference* (New York: Vintage, 2002).

Electoral Commission. Scottish Independence Referendum: Report On the Referendum Held On 18 September 2014. ELC/2014/02. Available at: http://www.electoralcommission.org.uk/__data/assets/pdf_file/0010/179812/Scottish-independence-referendum-report.pdf.

Evans, G. *Educational Failure and Working Class White Children in Britain* (London: Palgrave Macmillan, 2006).

Farrington, J. CIPFA stats show drops in library numbers and usage, *The Bookseller* (8 December 2014). Available at: http://www.thebookseller.com/news/cipfa-stats-show-drops-library-numbers-and-usage.

Flood, A. Readers absorb less on Kindles than on paper, study finds, *The Guardian* (19 August 2014). Available at: http://www.theguardian.com/books/2014/aug/19/readers-absorb-less-kindles-paper-study-plot-ereader-digitisation.

Flood, A. Library usage falls significantly as services shrink, *The Guardian* (10 December 2014). Available at: http://www.theguardian.com/books/2014/dec/10/library-usage-falls-dramatically-services-visits-down-40m.

Flood, A. Sharp decline in children reading for pleasure, survey finds, *The Guardian* (9 January 2015). Available at: http://www.theguardian.com/books/2015/jan/09/decline-children-reading-pleasure-survey.

Flood, A. Sales of printed books fall by more than £150m in five years, *The Guardian* (13 January 2015). Available at: http://www.theguardian.com/books/2015/jan/13/sales-printed-books-fell-150m--five-years.

Flouri, E. and Buchanan, A. Early father's and mother's involvement and child's later educational outcomes, *British Journal of Educational Psychology* 74: 141–153.

Frazier, I. *Gone to New York: Adventures in the City* (London: Granta, 2006).

Furedi, F. *Power of Reading: From Socrates to Twitter* (London: Bloomsbury, 2015).

Gallagher, K. *Reading Reasons: Motivational Mini-Lessons for Middle and High School* (Maine, NY: Stenhouse Publishers, 2003).

Gallagher, K. *Deeper Reading: Comprehending Challenging Texts, 4–12* (Maine, NY: Stenhouse Publishers, 2004).

Gallagher, K. *Readicide: How Schools Are Killing Reading and What You Can Do About It* (Maine, NY: Stenhouse Publishers, 2009).

Gardener, L. A Kindle in the classroom: e-reading devices and reading habits, *Language Arts Journal of Michigan* 27(1) (fall 2011). Available at: https://core.ac.uk/download/pdf/10684690.pdf.

Greenfield, S. *Mind Change: How Digital Technologies Are Leaving Their Mark On Our Brains* [Kindle edn] (London: Ebury, 2015).

Hamilton, E. W. *Raising Bookworms: Getting Kids Reading for Pleasure and Empowerment* (New York: Beech Tree Books, 2009).

Hicks, B. *Love All the People: Letters, Lyrics, Routines* (London: Constable & Robinson, 2005).

Hill, S. *Howard's End Is On the Landing: A Year of Reading from Home* [Kindle edn] (London: Profile Books, 2010).

Jacobs, A. *The Pleasures of Reading In An Age of Distraction* (New York: Oxford University Press, 2011).

Layne, S. L. *Igniting a Passion for Reading: Successful Strategies for Building Lifetime Readers* (Maine, NY: Stenhouse Publishers, 2009).

Lee, H. *To Kill a Mockingbird* (London: Pan Books, 1974).

Lewis, M. and Samuels, S. J. Read More, Read Better? A Meta-Analysis of the Literature On the Relationship Between Exposure to Reading and Reading Achievement. Unpublished manuscript, University of Minnesota, 2005.

Manguel, A. *A Reading Diary: A Year of Favourite Books* (Edinburgh: Canongate, 2006).

Manguel, A. *The Library At Night* (New Haven, CT: Yale University Press, 2009).

Manguel, A. *A Reader on Reading* (New Haven, CT: Yale University Press, 2010).

Manguel, A. *A History of Reading* (New York: Penguin, 2014).

McRae, A. and Guthrie, J. T. Promoting reasons for reading: teacher practices that impact motivation, in E. H. Hiebert (ed.), *Reading More, Reading Better* (New York: Guilford Press, 2009), pp. 55–76.

Miller, A. *The Year of Reading Dangerously: How Fifty Great Books Saved My Life* (London: Fourth Estate, 2014).

Miller, D. *The Book Whisperer: Awakening the Inner Reader in Every Child* (San Francisco, CA: Jossey-Bass, 2009).

Miller, D. *Reading in the Wild: The Book Whisperer's Keys to Cultivating Lifelong Reading Habits* (San Francisco, CA: Jossey-Bass, 2014).

Morretta, T.M. and Ambrosini, M. *Practical Approaches for teaching Reading and Writing in Middle Schools* (Newark, DE: International Reading Association, 2000).

Newark, T. *The Art of Slow Reading: Six Time-Honored Practices for Engagement* (Portsmouth, NH: Heinemann, 2012).

Newkirk, T. *Holding On to Good Ideas In a Time of Bad Ones: Six Literacy Principles Worth Fighting For* (Portsmouth, NH: Heinemann, 2009).

Pennac, D. *The Rights of the Reader* (London: Walker Books, 2006).

Pennac, D. *School Blues* (London: Maclehose Press, 2007).

Plato. *The Collected Dialogues of Plato*, ed. E. Hamilton and H. Cairns (Princeton, NJ: Princeton University Press, 1961).

Princeton University. The E-reader Pilot at Princeton: Final Report (Executive Summary) (fall 2009). Available at: https://www.princeton.edu/ereaderpilot/eReaderFinalReportShort.pdf.

Read On. Get On Campaign. *Read On. Get On: A Mission to Ensure ALL Children in Scotland Are Reading Well By 11* (London: Save the Children, 2014). Available at: http://www.savethechildren.org.uk/sites/default/files/docs/Read_On_Get_On_Scotland.pdf.

Ritchie, C. How much is a school librarian worth? *Library and Information Update* (May 2009). Available at: http://www.cis.strath.ac.uk/cis/research/publications/papers/strath_cis_publication_2376.pdf.

Roberts, H. *Oops! Helping Children Learn Accidentally* (Carmarthen: Independent Thinking Press, 2012).

Scottish Government. *Curriculum for Excellence. Building the Curriculum 3: A Framework for Learning and Teaching* (Edinburgh: Scottish Government, 2008). Available at: http://www.educationscotland.gov.uk/learningandteaching/thecurriculum/whatiscurriculumforexcellence/index.asp.

Scottish Government. Scottish Survey of Literacy and Numeracy 2014 (Literacy). Statistics Publication Notice. Available at: http://www.gov.scot/Resource/0047/00475898.pdf.

Sebald, W. G. *Austerlitz* (London: Penguin, 2001).

Senior, C. *Getting the Buggers to Read* (London: Continuum, 2008).

Smith, M. and Wilhelm, J. D. *Reading Don't Fix No Chevys: Literacy in the Lives of Young Men* (Portsmouth, NH: Heinemann, 2002).

Spufford, F. *The Child That Books Built* (London: Faber & Faber, 2002).

Statista. Statistics and facts on libraries in the United Kingdom (n.d.). Available at: http://www.statista.com/topics/1838/libraries-in-the-uk/.

Trotman, A. Kindle sales have 'disappeared', says UK's largest book retailer, *The Telegraph* (6 January 2015). Available at: http://www.telegraph.co.uk/finance/newsbysector/retailandconsumer/11328570/Kindle-sales-have-disappeared-says-UKs-largest-book-retailer.html.

United Nations. Secretary-general stresses need for political will and resources to meet challenge of fight against illiteracy (press release, 8 September 1997). Available at: http://www.un.org/press/en/1997/19970904.SGSM6316.html.

Williams, M. Pupils to help run libraries as full-time staff face axe, *The Herald* (11 November 2014). Available at: http://www.heraldscotland.com/news/13188910. Pupils_to_help_run_libraries_as_full_time_staff_face_axe/.

Willingham, D. T. *Raising Kids Who Read: What Parents and Teachers Can Do* (San Francisco, CA: Jossey-Bass, 2015).

Wilson, G. *Breaking Through Barriers to Boys' Achievement: Developing a Caring Masculinity*, 2nd edn (London: Bloomsbury, 2013).

Wolf, M. *Proust and the Squid: The Story and Science of the Reading Brain* (Cambridge: Icon Books, 2008).

Zaid, G. *So Many Books: Reading and Publishing In An Age of Abundance*, tr. N. Wimmer (London: Sort of Books, 2004).

INDEX

Socrates 65–67, 83, 138
Soltysek, Raymond 104
Standovich, K. E. 121
sweetcorn 8

T

technology 42, 68, 71, 96, 106 *see also* e-reader, Internet
The Rights of the Reader 33, 84, 127, 130, 131
Trotman, A. 41, 73

U

United Nations 127

W

War Games 4
Willingham, D. T. 23, 49
Wilson, G. 88, 119, 120
Wolf, M. 20, 23, 24, 43, 66

Z

Zaid, G. 20

Literacy
Commas, colons, connectives and conjunctions

ISBN: 978-178135128-4

Literacy is important. This book is about getting it right.

Its author is an expert in teaching children how to speak and write well, and has transformed the oral and written communication skills of many thousands of students. In *Literacy* he shares how he does it and what he knows about this most important of all skills and reveals what every teacher needs to know in order to radically transform literacy standards across the curriculum. The stories, anecdotes and insights into the many practical activities in this book are, in turn, and often in the same sentence, heart breaking, inspiring, shocking and, as ever, funnier and more readable than those in an education book have any right to be.

Contains everything teachers need to know to teach literacy effectively, regardless of their subject specialism or phase. If you want to make sure that every child leaves your class knowing the rules and how to use them, this is the book for you. If you think that literacy is difficult, or boring, or not your responsibility, be ready to be proved wrong. Discover practical activities, spelling strategies, tips for teaching punctuation and grammar guides that are anything but didactic and dull.